I'r tlodion (for the poor)

Hi Deb
Thanks a lot for getting this book
Hope you enjoy it.
Thanks james.

CONTENTS

Dedication

Foreword

Chapter 1: Harddwch (Beauty)   1

Chapter 2: Gobaith (Hope)   16

Chapter 3: Llechi (Slate)   32

Chapter 4: Gwaith (Work)   43

Chapter 5: Cariad (Love)   57

Chapter 6: Y wraigyn y gadairolwyn (The woman in the wheelchair)   75

Chapter 7: Ffrind (A friend)   83

Chapter 8: Fy Mrawd (My brother)   92

Chapter 9: Galar (Grief)   116

Chapter 10: Y Dailen (The leaves)   121

Chapter 11: Casau (Hate)   130

Chapter 12: Y brenhinoedd moch (The pig kings)   144

Chapter 13: Ymarfer (Practice)   149

Chapter 14: Paratoi (Preparation)   159

Chapter 15: Y Taith (The journey)   169

Chapter 16 - Y Morrigan   177

Chapter 17: Newid (Change)   194

Chapter 18: Y Diwedd (The end)   199

FOREWORD

This book has been a form of catharsis for me. I'm sure I'm not alone in being profoundly pissed off with the state of politics the last few years, where lying and foodbanks have become the new normal. There is something quite obscene about having profoundly rich tax avoiders in power who pushed austerity which hit the poorest in society the hardest.

There is a strong theme of inequality, with middle class families who own a home and have savings often having hundreds to thousands of times more wealth than people from the poorer working class side. It looks at the lack of aspiration which can run alongside it, how people often percieve you, not giving a shit about health and how easy it is to end of 'down and out'.

It is also something of a homage to North Wales, to some of its landscapes, some of its history, and to some of its awesome communities and language that can be found here. Where socialism still holds strong.

The book follows a rough timeframe of reality, for instance with Welsh devolution, the Iraq War, the Finacial crash and the cuts that followed. Outside of this the book is both from personal experiences and a very bent imagination. Having worked for the BMC (Britsh Mountaineering Council) as their Youth and Equity Officer I spent some time working with their Equity Steering Group, looking at reducing barriers to participation for under represented groups. An obvious barrier to families was the cost and people with a disability have often been hit hardest by austerity, hence the theme for one of the main characters and their thoughts and feelings when pushed to using a foodbank.

The Dinorwic slate quarry plays a large part in the book, where I've spent a vast number of days climbing and exploring, alone and with friends. There is the odd rave in the book and it tries to capture that feeling of dancing with friends, lost in music, maybe even hooking up with someone. As a keen rock climber I decided to throw in a bit of this too.

I see the book as a dark tragedy, comedy and something of a tongue in cheek picture of how I'd like to see some of the no good leaders of the world leave the stage.

Massive thanks to Maisy Lovatt for the stellar cover, Sophie Eleri James for outstanding proof reading and for the confidence. Mcmanus, Aggie, Heather, Will, Bransby for feedback on drafts and for Milo and Jez for inspiring me to get started.

I hope the book makes you laugh.

Cheers James

CHAPTER 1:
HARDDWCH (BEAUTY)

It was beautiful. A beautiful place, a beautiful start.

Although, some would argue against the village of Deiniolen being deemed as such. Nestled on the lower slopes of ElidirFawr, one of the largest mountains in Wales, Deiniolen was a village with a view. Looking out to the large island of Ynys Môn (Anglesey) with the Menai Straits slitting into the Irish Sea and the mountains of Eyryi (snowdonia) at its back. Much of the village boasted a view of the highest mountain in Wales, Yr Wyddfa (known as Snowdon to the tourists), with its neighbour Crib Goch often testament to its name in the setting sun, glowing red. Eleri had wavy black hair to her shoulders, sharp blue eyes for one so young and a noticeable 'unearthly' level of high energy. Members of her family struggled to keep up with her wanting to stay awake late at night to play games or craving social interaction. Eleri and her family had strong links with Deiniolen and its neighboring Quarry.

The huge slate quarry on the side of ElidirFawr, Dinorwic Quarry, had been important for employment in the village and in the 1830s was one of the biggest quarries in the world. When it shut in 1969, it left Deiniolen dealing with post-industrial issues common across the world; poverty, shops and pubs closing, and plenty of drugs. Eleri's father Ray had told her it had closed due to increased Health and Safety requirements, new materials becoming available for roofing, and competition via cheaper slates from abroad. Eleri thought it was a good thing

1

it had shut as working in it sounded profoundly dangerous.

Deiniolen was composed of terraced houses bunched loosely around the main road cutting West to East, before eventually curving South as it left the village and curved round to a dead end at Bus Stop Quarry, a small section of the huge quarry system. Eleri lived on the Eastern end of the village in an end of terrace house with her teulu (family). Most families in the village, including theirs spoke Welsh as their first language.

Her dad Ray was short, 5.7, and had dark, curly hair that reached his shoulders, brown twinkling eyes, rarely had a smile off his face and never took life too seriously. He had a job in a factory in the nearby town of Llanberis, which made climbing and forestry equipment by the name of DMM. Ray loved the environment that he lived in, and Eleri thought he knew the name of every plant and flower in Wales.

Eleri's mum Gwawr seemed a force of nature, with long blond hair, piercing blue eyes and a little shorter than Ray. She worked part time in a local café, Pete's Eats, cleaned some houses and was a keen campaigner for Plaid Cymru, whose founder Hugh R Jones was also notably from Deiniolen. Gwawr was a proud woman with deep roots in the land. Her father, Dafydd, had worked in the quarry and his father Hen (old) Dafydd before him. Gwawr would usually wear her favourite brown leather boots which stretched to just below her knees, tight jeans and an assortment of cool woollen jumpers.

Eleri had an older sister Megan, only 3 years difference and who looked like a mini version of Gwawr but with a more ready smile that she must have got off Ray. Eleri shared a room with Megan and loved it. They were thick as thieves and would often get told off by Gwawr for playing *Blur* and *Oasis* too loudly. Ray never said anything as he also got told off for having *Prodigy* and *Guns N' Roses* on even louder! He was particularly fond of tunes from 'Jilted Generation' and far too often 'Sweet Child of Mine'.

Last of the teulu was the little brother, Jordan. With dark, wild hair and a cheeky grin, he was always up to mischief and when feeling left out would try to get into Eleri and Megan's room before one or both kicked him back out. Although occasionally they let him linger, this was only to taunt him into playing piggy in the middle, throwing a ball above his head between them, a bit out of his reach. For Gwawr, Jordan was a little golden boy who could do no wrong.

The house that they lived in was a classic quarryman's terraced cottage, faced with large stones on the exterior, a slate roof, thick walls and with life centred around its living room, which held the fire and the heat. It was Eleri's job to set the fire each day which was necessary for any hot water. Eleri would lay on her belly in front of the fire like a cat and watch TV, with Jordan sometimes vying for her position. Eleri would normally just tickle him until he moved.

Eleri and Megan had a double decker bed in their room and Eleri felt like she owed Megan for letting her have the top bunk. On the wall opposite the bed was a picture of them and many of the children in Deiniolen at the Eisteddfod in Ebenezer chapel. The Eisteddfod was an annual event which most kids looked forward to in the village, with music, dancing and cool artwork, although the poetry was lost on Eleri.

There was also a dark pencil drawing of a menacing looking 'witch', with ravens flying around her. This was the Morrigan, a banshee creature her mum and dad told them tales about, the Goddess of war, fate and death. Eleri's good friend Isabelle had drawn it for her. Gwawr and Ray would often read stories from the Mabinogioin to the children before bed Both Eleri and Megan were intrigued by the idea of Morrigan, who Gwawr said was 'one of the dark goddesses of neopaganism'...whatever that meant. Eleri would sometimes jump off her bunk, onto Megan, pretending to be Morrigan, although Megan would often come out trumps in the wrestling match which ensued.

Eleri had heard her parents having a conversation about the Mabinogion when they thought she was asleep, and her and Megan had sneaked up to their bedroom door. They didn't fully understand what was being said, but it was clear Gwawr was keen on Ray missing out some parts of the book.

Gwawr: "I don't want us telling some parts of it Ray. What about the end of 'The dreams of emperor Maxen' where Cynan and his group talk about cutting out the tongues of women, lest their own language be corrupted. Or where Peredur's mother says, 'if you see a beautiful lady make love to her even if she does not want you, it will make you a better and braver man'. And what the hell happens at the end of the second branch? Where it says no one was left alive in Ireland apart from 5 pregnant women who give birth to sons who sleep promiscuously with their mothers? These parts sound pretty bloody dodgy to me; I don't want our kids getting lessons in morality like this."

Ray: "You make good points, we should leave these bits out eh. At least Peredur didn't take his mum's advice. Whoever wrote the part about Ireland must have had a bad experience with an Irishman. The stories written in the Mabinogion are very very old, even 50 years ago a lot of the world had much more bigoted views."

Gwawr: "Most places weren't chatting about cutting women's tongues out or encouraging rape."

Ray: "I always change the stories abit; the Morrigan isn't even in the Mabi really."

Gwawr: "We need the Morrigan in there as a kind of feminine heroine, otherwise it's just a load of blokes having dubious adventures."

Eleri and Megan's eyebrows rose at what they were hearing, and they shot back to their room when their dad came towards the door on his way to the toilet.

Jordan had a small room with a huge cupboard, which was

once a pantry, but now served as his den and was his main abode. It was full of dismantled electrical 'bits'; transistors, capacitors, circuit boards and micro-chips. Jordan loved taking things apart and would do so on anything he found, old TVs, Walkmans and he clearly didn't have a clue about what the parts did, but it had become a real hobby. He said that he wanted to become an inventor, but Eleri thought he'd need to learn how to put things back together if he was to stand any chance. Both Gwawr and Ray would keep a close eye on him if he started looking at any appliance in the house too closely, fearing, at worst, his electrocution and at best a loss of a key appliance.

On Sundays they would sometimes go for a family walk, a regular one being a circular loop, down through the sessile oak woodland in Fachwen to Llanberis, around Llyn Padarn (lake) and back up an assortment of paths which toured up the hillside to their house. Stinky goats could sometimes be seen and smelt. The larger goats gave Eleri the fear, intimidating beasts with huge horns which looked like they could do damage and that were unpeterbed by people. A field on the outskirts of Llanberis, next to the llyn, was a popular picnic stop for them on these walks.

Gwawr would chat about her dad, Dafydd, and her grandfather working as quarrymen, blowing up big walls of slate and having epics getting the stuff back down to Gilfach Ddu (black forge).They could see the forge from their picnic spot, with its huge waterwheel that was no longer in operation. Gwawr would also go into some of the quarry owners, such as Penrhyn, being rotten bastards who exploited the workers. None of the youths had met Dafydd nor his dad, both of whom had passed away having had complex health issues concerning inhaling the slate dust for years.

Ray would point out various mosses, plants and trees; Star Moss, Fern Moss, insectivorous plants like Sundew and Butterwort and the impressive Rowan trees which managed to grow on their own on big slate heaps. He showed them Map Lichen also known as Geographicum, which was the green lichen which was all over slate walls. He said it grew about 1cm a decade in radius, so you could work out how old bits of it were. In Yr Gwanwyn (the Spring) there were loads of tiny white flowers everywhere which Eleri loved and Ray told her that this was Bedstraw.

Gwawr and Ray would sometimes discuss politics:

Ray: "Plaid Cymru are all well and good for the Welsh language movement, but they'll weaken labour against the Tories then where will that leave us workers?"

Gwawr: "Labour don't care about the Welsh; it's all run by posh boys in London. Plaid is the party of Wales and for the Welsh. The founder was from Deiniolen for God's sake, and Tony Blair is English, and posh!"

Ray: "Gordon Brown is from Scotland though."

Gwawr: "He should join the SNP then!"

Eleri didn't fully follow the conversations such as these at the time, but it became clear that although her parents supported different political parties, they both disliked the Tory party big time. They called it the 'party against the poor'. Eleri didn't like the sound of this party either and hoped she'd never have to meet a Tory or someone who supported them. Megan was adamant that one day she'd be leader of Plaid Cymru, and Eleri would declare that a banshee was much more powerful than any leader of a political party.

Not including their parents, Eleri, Megan and Jordan had little to do with adults, apart from Thomas of course. Thomas was Ray's best friend who would often come around to watch the rugby and every time he came he would dish out skittles, mini eggs and such like to the kids. Thomas lived on his own at the other end of the village and drove the Number 85 bus between Llanberis and Bangor, which went through most of the villages between. He was a heavy-set man with short black hair, a gravelly voice and normally sported a red hoodie. Thomas and Ray had known each other since primary school and had been friends for more than 30 years. He had a slight limp in his right leg from his time when he was training to become a marine; the heavy loads they ran around with injured his knee badly and put paid to that career option. He was gutted for some years afterwards. Ray was at least glad to have Thomas as the bus driver, as he couldn't drive and he liked having chats with Thomas on the bus he used this to get to work in Llanberis.

He would often moan to Gwawr and Ray about his inability to get a girlfriend. Eleri thought it may be because he smoked so heavily, rarely seen without a rollie in his mouth. The children's eyes always hurt with all the smoke in the living room when he was there, but because he brought them sweets, they forgave him his vice. Thomas seemed to know everyone in the area, as most people had needed to use his bus at some point, and he was very chatty.

Gwawr and Ray were much amused by some of Thomas' efforts at relationships.

Thomas: "We were in the pub and I can't remember what I said to her but she went nuts and I was embarrassed about having a big argument with loads of pub goers watching. I ended up running outside getting into my small Clio and driving off as rapidly as possible. I headed out of town towards the Llanberis Pass and when I looked in my wing mirror I was shocked and scared to see she was giving chase. Worse still, she had a faster car and was hot on my heels. We had a crazy car chase until I ended up hobbling as fast as I could up the north ridge of Tryfan to escape, think I dossed somewhere on that mountain that night".

Stories such as these were not uncommon.

Jordan was very fond of Thomas, as Thomas would often pick him up and chuck him in the air to near the ceiling shouting, "you're Peter Pan!" Thomas was an extended part of the family and Gwawr would always try to give him seconds and even thirds of her homemade Cawl.

They'd watched the film 'Willow' at least three times together. It starred Warwick Davis and Val Kilmer and had sorcerers and evil witches. Eleri and Megan had a crush on Val Kilmer, called Mad Mardigan in the film. Best of all, a fair amount of the film was based in North Wales in Dinorwic Quarry, and Thomas would tell them stories about ferrying some of the actors about on the bus. He spoke about how he was gutted to miss out on being one of the horsemen, as they'd done a shout out in the Heights pub in Llanberis for extras. He laughed about how you'd not get away with Health and Safety wise of having people with no experience slotted onto horses for a film nowadays.

Eleri, Megan and Jordan went to school at Ysgol Gwaun Gynfi, on the Western end of Deiniolen. They were all in separate classes, with the school having around 150 pupils, split into 7 classes. Eleri thought school was 'ok', but much preferred the games they played during break times than any actual lessons. She also understood quickly that for some kids, school could be hell.

Deiniolen was a fairly poor village in comparison to most others in the UK, but at every school there is the 'poorest'. At Gwaun Gynfi (school) this was Matthew Vasquez, who was in the same class as Eleri. About the same age as Eleri, Matthew always looked unkempt, thin, badly washed and in worse clothing than everyone else. He already had a set of false teeth, and when he took them out and put them on the desk it fascinated Eleri, but disgusted some of the other kids.

The police were often round at Matthew's house, as his older brothers Daniel and Gareth were always getting into trouble. Their parents didn't seem to be bothered or get involved in the trouble themselves. If anyone had their houses burgled, or things disappear from their cars, the police normally knew where to go looking.

In break times Matthew didn't play with any of the kids, just hung out on his own and was hard to approach. Eleri had tried a few times...

Eleri: "You should join in our game of tig Matt, you look fast!"

Matthew: "I don't think so, thanks though. I try to get away from my brothers, but they always catch me."

Eleri: "Well if you change your mind, you can join any time."

He never did.

It was the first time Eleri got to observe bullying on a day-to-day basis, mainly directed at Matthew. As he looked different, was the slowest learner in the school and had family issues that most kids knew about outside school, he was an obvious target.

Some kids would chant "tramp, tramp, tramp" at break times when the teachers weren't watching.

He was always getting quizzed in a mean way from other kids in class.

Georgina Booth asked him "are you stupid?" Georgina seemed posh and stuck up to Eleri.

John Hudson sneered at Matthew and asked "have you been burgling houses, like your brothers? You'll be locked up soon too".

The barrage of snide comments and behaviours were every hour, every day and even the teachers seemed to join in. Their main teacher Glyn Williams a bespeckled owl of a man, often struggled with Matthew, not knowing how to bring him up to speed with the rest of the class. He sometimes whispered his thoughts loudly, almost unconsciously, but where everyone could hear; "You'll struggle to get anywhere in life, Matthew".

Eleri had told the other kids to stop when they were being mean, but most weeks Matthew was still clearly taking an avalanche of shit day-to-day. Eventually he bunked off school for months. They brought him back in for a couple of weeks sometime later, and some of the teachers told him off. After these two weeks, he left for good, and Eleri never saw or heard from Matthew again. She'd never managed to become Matthew's friend, but missed having him and his false teeth in her class and felt that an injustice had been served in life.

It made her think that a person's postcode and the household they were born into was likely to dictate many of life's outcomes.

She heard Georgina and John chatting amongst themselves and their friends:

John: "Smelly, dirty little sod's gone. Good."

Georgina: "Maybe he's got a job as a wheelie bin!"

Eleri cut them off: "You two are really mean! You can see he's had no luck in his life and is having a hard time, how would you like to be in his position".

They looked shocked before inferring that Eleri had fancied him. Her dealings with them over the next few years were never warm.

Her two main friends in school were Isabelle Smith and Zoe Bud.

Isabelle had a face that reminded Eleri of the moon. With an ever-present big smile, overlaid with long curly dark hair, she was already an artist of sorts, making jewellery and even selling some postcards with some drawings she made in some local cafes. Although only 10 years old she was already the trendiest person in Deiniolen and lived directly opposite the school on the high street.

Zoe was a bit taller than Eleri and Isabelle, with short shoulder length hair and usually had a knowing smirk, like she knew something about you that you'd done wrong. She wore the same blue tracksuit all the time. Blue suited her. Zoe lived a mile up the hill out of town, up in Dinorwic.

They'd sometimes have sleepovers at each other's houses.

Isabelle's bedroom was full of drawings she was working on and had a huge dreamcatcher by her bed, she was adamant that the bigger it was, the more likely it would catch dreams. Her mum, Bella, had the same smiling face and made the best bara brith, although she got a bit of stick off people for not being from Wales. She was trying to learn Welsh and it was funny watching an adult struggling with a language all the kids found easy. Bella had one of the few computers in the village, a PC 286, and knew a way of writing she called shorthand which looked like Egyptian hieroglyphics to Eleri. Isabelle had learned some of it too.

Zoe's parents had split up not too long ago. Her parents Anita and Gareth still seemed to get on well and Eleri liked them both, although it was normally Anita's house in Dinorwic that they would stay over at. Anita seemed a remarkably understanding woman, and Eleri and Isabelle were always on best behaviour when at the house out of respect for how nice Anita was. She was also an expert carpenter and had a small workshop on the side of her house. She was well-known in the area for making driftwood kitchens and tables which were much sought after. Zoe said her mum worked super hard and could lose herself in her workshop for hours and hours. Whereas she said her dad Gareth was a proper slacker. Gareth had moved to the top of Goodman Street in Llanberis when he moved out, which Eleri figured would be handy for chumming in some of the cafes where he often loitered. Apparently, he did some sort of journalistic work for the Welsh Tourist Board and seemed to spend a lot of his time rock climbing and cavorting after women.

Zoe had posters of Jordan and Danny from New Kids on the Block on her wall, and forced Eleri and Isabelle to listen to the boy band for at least half an hour every time they were round.

As Ray didn't have a driving license, it fell to Gwawr to ferry people around as needs be in the amazingly rusted, golden coloured '1986' Nissan Cherry. The oft damp climate of North-West Wales wasn't ideal for the health of vehicles and it often took Gwawr 20 minutes to get the car started. Spraying WD40 onto something inside the engine and spending a bit of time swearing at the car seemed to do the job.

Some Saturdays, Gwawr would take the family to do a big shop in Bangor, the local City, she'd also love to go hunting through charity shops. It was a 20 minute drive from Deiniolen. She never let on what it was she was looking for, but occasionally random items would be bought; a bowl, the odd jumper for one of the kids. By the end of the circuit through town, Eleri was the only one of them without tired legs. When the weather was good Gwawr would treat them to an ice cream after the marathon charity shop tour and they'd sit on one of the wooden benches next to the beautiful sandstone Cathedral in the centre. Jordan would put a small bit of ice cream on his nose and try to lick it off much to everyone's amusement.

Ray would normally avoid these 'sessions' and the one time he did join them, Eleri thought he looked glum. She figured he'd prefer to be watching the rugby with Thomas, or socialising in the pub. She was glad when he joined them though.

In some of the better winters they'd get enough snow that the school would close, and they'd go sledging in the steep fields above the village. Once, Ray managed to get Megan, Eleri and Jordan onto the same sled and sent them sailing downwards, snow spraying into all their faces and Jordan screaming his head off. One time they hit a rock hidden by the snow when going pretty fast and they all got catapulted off the sledge and were nursing sore bums for the rest of the day. Gwawr gave Ray some earache for the crash.

Yr Haf (Summer) was Eleri's favourite time of year; long days, sunny-ish and when it got hot enough, Gwawr and Ray would even take them all nofio (swimming) in Llyn Padarn. There was a small train on one side of the lake which took tourists 2km along the lake, then back the same way. This side of the lake was usually quiet when the train wasn't running and had plenty of smooth rock spurs fingering into the water; a perfect area for families to dwell for a while. Ray and Gwawr had to look after Jordan in the water, who couldn't swim properly without arm bands, but Eleri and Megan were free to be 'mermaids'. Thomas would come down with beers but never went in the water, claiming it wasn't 'natural'. He just sat smoking and drinking on the side. Eleri liked to swim underwater and hold her breath, then grab Jordan by the leg to scare him. There was the odd canoe on the Llyn, some with children overseen by an adult, and some boats with older kids or adults sporting alcoholic beverages.

On one day while they were swimming a man walked past who looked the most unhappy person Eleri had ever seen. He was stocky with long blondish/grey hair, a heavily wrinkled face and a mouth arched like a dark rainbow across his face, the picture of deep sorrow. There was silence from everyone but Jordan when he was near. Once he was past, Thomas piped up:

Thomas: "That's Smiler, he's been like that since his kid committed suicide."

Gwawr: "Let's not talk about this now Thomas."

Jordan: "What does committed suicide mean?"

Gwawr whispered: "Here we go", then; "It's when people are very unhappy and don't enjoy being here anymore, so they go."

Jordan: "Where do they go?"

Gwawr: "Where we all go when we die, into the ground."

Jordan: "I don't want to go into the ground, I don't know why anyone would want to either."

Gwawr smiled at this and pushed him into the water to take his mind off it. Eleri watched Smiler walk away, still intrigued by the deep sorrow which was buried in his face. Ray and Thomas also looked solemn. Eleri wondered what events and bad luck must come to pass in someone's life for them to want to commit suicide, and her only experience of this was Matthew's poor treatment in school.

Late one summer, there were large celebrations in most local towns and villages after a 'Welsh devolution referendum' which supported a formation for a National Assembly for Wales. Eleri remembered eating a lot of fairy cakes at school and her mum telling her that it was a stepping-stone towards becoming fully independent. Ray just said it was a good thing and that the Labour Party had made it all possible. Gwawr rolled her eyes at this but with a darkening face added: "the Conservative Party were the only major political party who opposed devolution."

During some of the celebrations the whole family had been in their local pub, The Bull, and then Gwawr had driven them up the road to near where the road ends around Bus Stop Quarry. They'd all walked along the good path leading into the middle of the huge quarry, which seemed to cleave into half of Elidir Fawr, itself a 3000 foot mountain. They walked for about 15 minutes to a section which stuck out towards Llanberis, and had an amazing 'lookout' point into the Llanberis pass. There were steep inclines here and there where the slate used to be lowered down. Incredible looking walls, often 30 or 40 feet high, would form the sides of these inclines.

The sun was low in the sky and cast a red glow across Crib Goch (the red ridge), with the iron pyrite helping to give it such a look. Jordan whooped, giddy with the cool summer breeze and views of the wild. Eleri jumped up onto Megan to get a piggyback, so they could enjoy the view together as one. They chatted at the lookout for half an hour watching the sun disappear from the mountain. On the walk out of the quarry a large Cigfran (raven) flew down out of the sky and perched on the top of a wall of an old quarry work shed. Eleri thought it was looking at her as they walked past and took it as a good omen, as the Morrigan, the banshee was also the goddess of Corvids.

Eleri thought it must be the most stunning place in the world and, with her family that she loved, she felt she must be the luckiest person.

CHAPTER 2:
GOBAITH (HOPE)

Things really appeared to be 'on the up'. Gwynedd, the county in which Eleri lived, was part of the European Union's Objective 1 programme. This was awarded to regions in Europe that achieved less than 75% of the EU average GDP. This helped support many rural industries, SMEs, lifelong learning opportunities and better transport links. The programme came from research showing that these regions with low average wages often had poor housing, ill health, low educational achievement and skill levels. Low disposable incomes had led to some areas experiencing social exclusion.

Eleri had discovered this when she started secondary school in Bangor at Ysgol Friars in her first week, thanks to her lovely and brilliant Geography teacher, Miss Smith. The EU's Objective 1 programme made a lot of sense to Eleri as she'd seen improvements even in Deiniolen. Lots of buildings had been improved with new pebble dash and nicely painted walls, a caffi had opened on the high street, and there were a few posters about adult learning opportunities. She was glad she knew what the EU's circle of stars plaques scattered around the area meant now, thanks to Miss Smith telling her.

Her sister Megan had been at Friars for over two years and had given Eleri a good idea about what to expect. She was very grateful that Zoe and Isabelle had been put in her form. Little Jordan was on his own back in Gwaun Gynfi in Deiniolen.

She soon found out that Megan had started to smoke at

breaktimes, in an area with trees where the teachers couldn't see them. Her boyfriend Cai had probably got her into it.

Eleri: "I thought you smelled funny when you got back home!"

Megan: "Sorry, it is a gross habit, the first few tasted horrendous too."

Eleri: "I want to try one."

Megan: "You will NOT! Mum would kill me for getting you into smoking."

Eleri: "I'll get one off someone else then."

Megan: "Don't do it Eleri. It's very addictive and you love running around. It doesn't do you any good, it makes running really hard, all that black tar going on your lungs too."

Eleri: "Why did you start to do it then if it's that bad?"

Megan: "Just for something to do, because some of my friends were doing it. Think I was stressed out in my first few weeks of school too, and it seemed a way of fitting in."

Eleri: "Those reasons sound daft if it's that bad."

Some weeks later, Zoe brought in a few cigarettes. She said she'd got them off her dad. In a circle with Isabelle, they lit a ciggy and Zoe passed it round. Each girl had a drag, their faces turning a pasty green as the hot poisonous gas went into their throat and lungs. They persevered quietly for 4 drags each before Zoe said:

"That's more than enough, its fucking awful!"

Isabelle started to say something but puked instead.

Although they had a grim first experience, like millions of others had before them, they persevered, and eventually even Megan would let them smoke in her and Cai's smoking area of the school grounds.

Much like in her first school, Eleri preferred breaktimes and PE over any of the sedentary lessons. However, she had an affinity for Geography, partly from Ray's teachings and partly because she liked her teacher. Miss Smith was in her late 20's, petit with very short ginger hair. She seemed to have travelled everywhere, with a large map of the world on her wall and drawing pins marking where she'd been.

Miss Smith: "Can anyone tell us how this valley was created? Yes, Eleri?" She was pointing to a picture of a valley somewhere in the Lake District on the classroom wall.

Eleri: "By glaciers miss, in the ice ages. You can tell because it's U-shaped."

Miss Smith: "Very good. Can anyone name some of the rock types found in our local, glacier made valleys? Eleri again?"

Eleri: "Slate, Rhyolite, Dolerite, volcanics, old Precambrian quartzite out on Anglesey."

Miss Smith:"Excellent stuff."

Miss Smith seemed particularly keen on teaching about inequality, around human geography:

"Exposure to poverty when people are young increases the risk of trauma later in life, with people often becoming less healthy, more prone to risky and criminal behaviours, having poor educational and academic outcomes and money issues. Food insecurity for children can be very bad, making them more likely to get ill. Disabled are also on the sharp end and are five times more likely to be at risk of poverty and food insecurity. Food insecurity at any age is linked to a higher probability of chronic illness. Examples of negative impacts can be memory difficulties, depression, gum disease, arterial disease, mental illness, diabetes, suicide. I could go on and on".

"Can anyone explain to me the difference between equity and

equality?"

John Smith, a smallish blonde boy, piped up: "Are they not the same thing Miss?"

Miss Smith shook her head slightly: "Most people think so, but they are not. Equality is giving everyone the same thing, equal opportunities so to speak, but equity is giving more to people who need it more and less to people who need it less. So, the tax system can actually be a pretty fair system, where someone who earns £15,000 a year pays a smaller share of tax than someone who earns £60,000 a year. However, some payments and taxes are inequitable, for instance VAT, at around 20% tax on all items. This has a more profound effect on poorer households than richer ones. The same as a TV license - for poorer households it takes a much higher percentage of their wealth and I believe this kind of cost should all be done though the tax system. Although a lot of people dread the word tax, it should just be called 'money for services' and for most developed nations the more you earn, the more you pay as a percentage of your earnings, up to a point for most where some of the less scrupulous rich use offshore accounts. I'd better not get started on those, or we'd be here all night."

When Eleri listened to some of Miss Smith's lectures on inequality, it filled her with a determination to try and do something about it somehow when she grew up. They made her look at things in a different way and made her realise many benefits available were aimed towards people with sufficient wealth who didn't require anything, whereas the truly poor were often silently penalised with only people such as Miss Smith paying it any heed. It also made her think back to Matthew, her classmate from a few years earlier and wondered about what his future held for him.

Eleri trusted Miss Smith. On one occasion she asked her to stay behind after class and offered some extra-curricular advice.

Miss Smith: "In the next few years Eleri, you may be offered the opportunity of getting a lift with someone who has drunk too much alcohol, please don't get in the car with them."

Eleri: "I won't Miss Smith, thanks for the advice though."

Miss Smith: "Good. I had a few friends have near misses and one, Helen Dawes, got seriously injured when getting driven home from a party by someone who was drunk. It's very dangerous, but can be hard to say no. It's always worth thinking about how you get home from these things."

Eleri: "Thomas, our family friend who drives the buses, has told us of a few stories with people who have been drunk. I think some have nearly got onto his bus."

Miss Smith: "Another point Eleri. You may end up taking things other than alcohol. If you do, be sure not to drink too much booze with it."

Eleri: "I think I know what you mean Miss." She didn't have a clue at the time.

Eleri made a few new friends at Friars. There were two in particular she would go onto spend a good deal of time with; Osian and Lewis. Osian Llewelyn had a wide face, the thickest glasses Eleri had ever seen, cool, curly blonde hair and thick arms. Osian lived within thirty minutes walking distance of the school in the village of Menai Bridge itself and spent much of his breaktime playing football, but would join Eleri, Zoe and Isabelle' for the odd ciggy. He was also a keen climber and would go to Maes Glas, an indoor climbing wall in Bangor, regularly, which might have explained his large arms. He was extremely good natured and friendly with everyone.

Lewis was pale, skinny as a rake, with long shaggy hair, a dour look and was also a keen climber, often joining Osian at

Maes Glas indoor wall. He lived a few miles along the coast which verged onto the Menai Straits, Y Felinheli. He was pretty introverted, Eleri thought, and harder to engage in conversation than Osian, but he clearly had a lot going on within all the scraggly hair, often coming out with shrewd observations when most people near him would have thought he was half asleep. Eleri had gone to the wall and seen them both climb. Osian looked brutally strong, whereas Lewis was obviously weaker but oozed confidence when he moved and was better on the vertical walls.

Osian invited Eleri, Zoe, Isabelle and Lewis to his 13th Birthday party at his house in Menai bridge. Zoe's mum Anita had dropped them all off on a Saturday afternoon, all ready for a buffet lunch. Osian's mum Elliw had put out sausage rolls, quiches, crisps and cakes, which went down a treat with the 12 other children who came. Osian's house seemed big to Eleri, 5 bedrooms, detached, with a big garden which had a pond in one corner and a large shed-come-conservatory, where his mum liked to work, editing science journals. His dad Glyn worked for the local council, something to do with social housing.

After the buffet, they all sang 'happy birthday' to Osian as Elliw brought in a huge chocolate cake with candles, which Osian swiftly blew out before messily slicing it up for everyone to get a piece. They all went out to the local park for a football match soon afterwards. Eleri remembered it being fun, but mainly remembered Isabelle going down when a girl called Charlie kicked her shin hard in a tackle. A heated exchange ensued before Osian de-escalated the situation, a handy gift to have for someone keen on football.

After that, Osian and Lewis would occasionally join them at their houses in Deiniolen and Dinorwic, although they gave the pyjama parties a miss. As well as working for the council, Osian's dad Glyn had a hobby crafting 'things' out of stone; a granite dragon which overlooked their pond, a huge slate sword the size of a person perched outside the workshop and waiting to be moved to the garden of the person who paid Glyn to make it. Osian said Elliw was pissed off because Glyn's new tools for working the stone were in *her* workshop. Osian had started to join his dad with this hobby, offering a bit of father and son time.

He became quite adept fairly quickly and when it was Eleri's 13th birthday, he walked past Gwawr to hand Eleri a piece of slate 2 feet long, 1 foot wide and 2 inches thick with her name engraved into it. Eleri gasped when Osian let her take it, not expecting how heavy it was. Everyone was very impressed and most wanted one of their own!

Lewis asked: "Can you make me one, I love slate."

Isabelle: "And me!"

Zoe: "Me too!"

Jordan: "Me too please, Osian!"

Osian: "Christ, it took me two weeks to make that, so it's going to be slow. I'll see what I can do, maybe for your birthdays."

True to his word, Osian did make them all one for their birthdays, be it smaller than the one he had made for Eleri. Jordan was delighted with his and put it at the entrance to his cupboard.

Jordan still enjoyed taking machines apart, although he'd gotten old enough to realise the appliances in the house were out of bounds. He didn't seem to enjoy school much, but Eleri could empathise with this.

Ray and Gwawr seemed in a good place from Eleri's perspective, a couple who worked well together and had fun. She knew it wasn't that way for all couples; some of the people she knew at school talked of terrible rows their parents had on a regular basis. Eleri wondered if they might be better off separating when relationships get to that stage.

It was around this time that 'something bad' started to occur on the news.

President Bush: "We believe they have weapons of mass destruction."

UN: "Wait for Hans Blix to do his investigation."

President Bush: "We are going to war and not waiting..."

Tony Blair: "We are joining America and going to war with Iraq..."

Both Gwawr and Ray hated the thought of this war. From what Eleri had learned about WW1 and WW2 she hated the idea of war too and didn't trust President Bush.

There was a huge anti-war protest lined up for London and a coach was leaving Llanberis to travel down. Gwawr and Ray got the whole family on board, with Lewis and Isabelle also in tow. It left at 5am, with around 50 bleary eyed people from the area on board and it took about five hours. Eleri was extremely pleased to see Miss Smith on the coach, marking some work on the way down, ever industrious. They smiled and waved at each other. They had one stop, where there were food stalls with this protest in mind selling very good cheap samosas and spicy things Eleri didn't really know the name of. As the coach arrived in the streets of London, Eleri was dumbfounded at the city's size and how many people seemed to be in it.

She wasn't sure exactly where they were dropped off, but the idea was to march through the streets and arrive at Hyde Park where some famous bands were going to play. Gwawr looked stressed trying to keep an eye on everyone and started instructing them all.

Gwawr: "Don't get out of my sight now, stay together. That includes you Ray."

Ray: "No worries, relax, this will be fun!"

Gwawr: "We could all get crushed in a crowd like this, especially Jordan."

Ray: "Nobody is going to get crushed."

Sue Wood, who organised the coach, ordered everyone to be back at the bus for 6pm at the absolute latest, or risk being left behind. Once that was said, their small family and friends team set off following the river-like flow of the crowd. There were people of all races and creeds, people beating drums, strumming guitars and endless voices, mainly shouting "STOP THE WAR", although sometimes using different words. Eleri loved the atmosphere, but Jordan got tired legs quickly and needed Ray to carry him for a while.

Most people seemed very friendly, but for a short while they were with a gang of more aggressive looking men in their 20's all chanting "DOWN, DOWN USA". Eleri figured that like her, they didn't trust President Bush either. Lewis and Isabelle took up the chant with them, until Gwawr hushed them, perhaps worrying it could instigate a crush.

At some point Ray pointed out the Houses of parliament, where the Government did its business.

After a few hours of hustling along, they eventually neared Hyde Park, only to be told that the music had ended. Eleri, Megan and Isabelle were a little underwhelmed at this news, but before they could think on it much, Gwawr realised they needed to hot-foot it back to the coach. Once the last stragglers were on board, Sue Wood hopped on and asked the driver to take them home. Many people were snoozing by the time it pulled up in Llanberis. Lewis' mum, Gwawr was waiting to pick him up, but Isabelle stayed over at Eleri's house.

The next day they watched the news and it said that there were over a million people at the protest. Jordan crowed out, "a million? So many!" It had footage from a helicopter with all the streets crammed with protesters. Eleri and Isabelle tried to spot themselves, but it was like trying to find a needle in a moving haystack. A short time later, and much to Eleri and her family's disappointment, Tony Blair declared that Britain was still going to join America in its war with Iraq.

The protest had failed and the Government hadn't listened to the people. Both Gwawr and Ray thought it was a terrible mistake and that it was more about oil reserves in Iraq than about Weapons of Mass Destruction. Soon after, the news was full of "shock and awe", helicopters, explosions and big black clouds of things burning. It was a depressing time, and Eleri felt that they were on the wrong side of history.

Outside of bombs and deaths on the other side of the world, Eleri felt that general life stuff was going well for her. She'd gotten into the habit of spending the first hour back from school doing her homework, and by applying herself for this hour, the classes in school started to feel both enjoyable and even easy, and many teachers complimented her on her work and knowledge.

After the hour of homework she went out for half an hour's jog most days. She also kept a meticulous diary she worked on at the end of each day, of things which needed doing and noteworthy occurrences and feelings, sometimes with pencil drawings to make it more animated.

Megan: "I wish I was like you. I hate doing homework and running looks hard work! I guess you don't smoke as much as me though..."

Eleri: "I'd just be watching TV otherwise and there is nothing I like between four and five."

Megan: "Most of the homework I get seems so dull, I leave it to last minute, if at all."

Eleri: "All the seconds we have seem small, but put together add up to a person's life. It's good to learn as much as we can, so we can make the world a better place. That's what Miss Smith thinks."

Megan: "I wish I had a teacher like her, a couple of mine seem like alcoholics! Mr Pratt the Chemistry teacher always seems to have a bottle of whisky in his desk and he stinks!"

Eleri: "Miss Smith says that some types of trauma in a person's life can lead to addictions. I wonder if that's a cause."

Megan: "I'd not thought of that. I feel sorry for him if that's the case."

During this phase of application, Eleri had started to squint a lot to read what teachers were writing on the blackboards at school. It all appeared blurry and would sometimes necessitate copying what was written off nearby classmates. This eventually led to a trip to the opticians, Alton Murphy's in Bangor, and glasses.

Eleri: "Will I need to wear these for long?"

Mr Jones, the optician, said in a fairly stern voice: "I'm afraid you will always need glasses now."

She wasn't too psyched on this at first and felt self-conscious, but the round silver-rimmed glasses soon became invisible to her and the odd mean comment of "speci 4 eyes" soon went stale. Zoe and Isabelle were the worst for teasing her about them.

Eleri did a good deal of reading around the schoolwork. Motivated particularly by Miss Smith's sense of morality, she read up on inequality. The Rowntree Foundation had plenty of interesting information and she felt it was very relevant for where she lived. A fair amount of it was very simple. The difference in wealth in someone who had a mortgage and owned a house in their lifetime, and someone who lived in rented accommodation all their lives created a huge rift between the two.

People who were super wealthy often dehumanised people from poorer backgrounds, sometimes hardly seeing them as human. People who were poorer, by and large, would pay a much higher percentage of tax during their lifetime than someone from a very wealthy background. Eleri was appalled at many of the points she found, and felt determined to do something about it. She started to have chats with Gwawr and Ray about it.

Eleri: "Which politicians are taking on inequality?"

Ray: "Labour politicians. They stand up for the unions, and they've helped to get a reasonable minimum wage, holidays, loads of stuff like that. Nye Bevan helped set up the NHS and the welfare state. He knew what it was to be poor; he was from a coal mining family and was a miner himself, *and* he was unemployed for years too. Gordon Brown also supports aid for Africa to reduce world inequality."

Gwawr: "I can tell you which ones are promoting inequality! The Conservative ones. They are all from old money, familial wealth. That is why they pay for private schools for their children, have offshore accounts to avoid tax, and argue for reducing taxes. They can pay for services such as private health care, and by reducing taxes this leads to reduced public services for the poor. This increases the divide between them and the poor."

Ray: "Hard to argue with that. The tax system can be used in a fair manner; the more you earn the more you should pay realistically, as you notice it less, but it's not how it works for the Tories. That's why nobody votes for the sods in Wales."

Eleri: "I like the sound of Nye Bevan."

Gwawr: "He was a great person; he'd definitely be Plaid Cymru if he was alive today."

Eleri: "Are we precariats? I read that's poor working class?"

Gwawr: "Possibly. We rent this house, but we own a car; a lot of people in the village can't afford that. We're lucky."

Eleri: "Could we buy the house?"

Ray: "Ha, not unless we sold you, Megan and Jordan, and

probably my liver and kidneys too."

Gwawr: "As far as I'm concerned, people who own a house are very fortunate indeed, investing money into something for themselves. We are just giving money to the council, who own this place."

Ray: "A lot better than living on the streets. You see a few homeless people in Bangor. I wonder what unlucky twists and turns in their poor lives took them there."

Eleri: "I hope Matthew from my old school doesn't end up like that."

Gwawr: "I'm sure he won't Eleri."

Eleri wasn't so sure from what she'd seen in school and what she'd been reading regarding life chances for the truly poor.

When Cai came around the house sometimes, Megan would ask Eleri to stay clear of their room when Gwawr and Ray were out of the house at work. She could hear scuffling sounds and figured they were playing a game. They'd usually go outside for a cigarette afterwards.

When Megan first mentioned that they'd been having sex at these times, Eleri was in total shock.

Eleri: "You what!? You've shagged him? Mum and dad would kill you if they found out!"

Megan: "No they wouldn't, everyone my age is doing it."

Eleri: "What's it like?

Megan: "Messy...but nice."

Eleri: "How nice?"

Megan smiled slightly smugly: "You'll have to wait until you find out."

Eleri grimaced. She wasn't convinced she'd want to if it was messy.

Thomas would still come around fairly regularly and, as usual, had tales of relationship epics, both his own and other people's within the area.

Thomas: "Gladys said she'd found out her partner Dougie had been having an affair, found some texts on his phone and said she went nuts. Kicked him out."

Gwawr: "I'd heard and I know who with. What a twat, eh, poor Gladys."

Thomas: "Yeah, poor Dougie too though. It's desperate splitting up."

Gwawr: "It's his fault though!"

Thomas: "Nobody knows what goes on between couples though, only them."

Gwawr: "It's pretty clear he's left his lovely wife for a bit of skank Thomas, everyone knows what she's like. People set themselves boundaries for good reason and she has none, wild is just another word for shithead."

Thomas: "I saw a counsellor in a relationship I was in once, keen as ever to try and keep one going longer than usual. The counsellor said that our childhood experiences shape what our behaviours are now. That's why I try not to blame anyone for how they are, as who can choose what happens to them when they are a child?"

Gwawr looked thoughtful for a minute, then continued slagging Dougie off as Thomas listened and puffed on his rollie.

Ray had gotten some sort of promotion in the DMM factory. To celebrate, they all went out for a bar meal in the Glyntwrog pub a mile down the road. Jordan's little face lit up with a smile when he got stuck into his fish fingers and beans, and Ray's did too when he started to down his pint of Hoegaarden. It made Eleri smirk at the pair of them.

Jordan: "Will we get more birthday presents now?"

Megan: "Yeah dad, what's in it for each of us?"

Ray laughed: "I'll let Gwawr decide how to spend the extra, otherwise it will all go on this." Ray pointed at his beer.

Gwawr: "Perhaps more books for you all to read."

Megan and Jordan both dejectedly said "oh" at the same time.

Books sounded fantastic to Eleri but what she could really use was a pair of rock boots because she had found another passion by hanging out with her friends, Lewis and Osian, and had gotten into rock climbing. She'd gone to Maes Glas indoor climbing wall with them a few times and had really started to love the movement, which felt like a game of chess. Working out how to do moves between holds, she had also started to build up her finger and arm strength.

Osian's dad, Glyn, had driven them to some outdoor boulders a few times in the Llanberis Pass and Ogwen valley, climbing above bouldering mats they'd borrowed from a local climbing wall. They went to Cromlech and Caseg Fraith areas, which were some really beautiful locations, and it all felt very different to climbing indoors. Lewis, who was into doing bigger climbs with ropes and equipment, pointed out some of the climbs he'd done on nearby crags. The climbs were given names.

Lewis: "Up there on Dinas Cromlech I did the crack on the right, it's called Cemetery Gates""

Osian was not into the bigger climbs and said: "It looks high and hard from here, good effort Lewis."

Lewis climbed slowly, as falling off on the bigger climbs could be dangerous, whereas Osian climbed fast and dynamically, so was good on the difficult and gymnastic short climbs they were doing above the bouldering pads. Eleri would definitely get Lewis to take her on some of the bigger climbs once she'd built her confidence on the smaller ones.

On one of these visits to Caseg Fraith, which offered a good view of Tryfan, a Welsh 3000 foot mountain, meaning the 3 peaks, with the middle peak being the tallest and having two large boulders known as Adam and Eve, bold walkers would make the small jump between the two. Lewis started to roll a joint. After sparking it, he duly offered it to Eleri and Osian. Being considerably larger than a normal ciggy, Eleri was glad she'd acclimatised to smoking before taking drags on the spliff, or she felt she might have puked like Isabelle. It gave her a warm feeling in her head and she felt mellow, but it definitely didn't do the afternoon's climbing productivity any good.

Eleri: "Thanks Lewis, where do you get the weed"

Lewis: "The skunk? My brother gives me it."

Osian: "That's alright isn't it, sound brother."

Lewis: "Yeah proper sound, Dan is, he lives in Bangor and there seems to be a bit of a crew of them who can sort out gear."

Feeling particularly high and buzzy, Eleri asked them both:

"What do you two want to be when you are older?"

Lewis: "Not sure, maybe work in conservation? With all the studies being done around global warming, it seems there'll be plenty of work needed to save the planet"

Osian: "Nice one Lewis, that sounds good. I'm enjoying stone craft at the moment, but not sure if I'll be able to make a living out of it," he said modestly. "What about you Eleri?"

Eleri: "I'd like to help make the world fairer. I've been reading stuff from the Rowntree Foundation, maybe I'd try to get some work with an organisation like that. It wouldn't be hard to do, would it, to help make policies which help reduce inequality?"

Lewis, Osian and Eleri smiled at their hopeful answers, feeling high as fuck.

CHAPTER 3:
LLECHI (SLATE)

The huge slate quarry in the side of the 3000-foot mountain, Elidir Fawr, was an integral part of the community, where many people's parents and relatives had laboured hard, and over 300 of them had died. After drilling the boreholes, they filled them with gunpowder and the three-minute fuses sometimes went off too quickly, blasting out the sharp slate shrapnel. If people hadn't made it into the three-foot-thick blast shelters, it was incredibly dangerous.

The slate rock type was effectively, compacted down mudstone. The sheer vertical cliffs created whilst quarrying could be, and often still are, very unstable, with huge chunks of slate, hundreds of tons in weight, sometimes falling away from the main mass of rock into chasms, giving a thunderous echo for miles around. Like slate versions of the ice seracs found on glaciers. At the base of the huge quarry lay a lake, Llyn Peris, and a large industrial complex which was part of a hydroelectric power station. This led into Elidir Fawr itself via huge tunnels and caverns, and through to a reservoir high on the other side of the mountain to Marchlyn Mawr.

Some of the reasonably sized quarry buildings were cegins (kitchen).Often, the oldest member working in that area of the quarry would have the job of keeping the kettle on for panads (cups of tea) for the quarrymen in their breaks. And breaks they did deserve, as the work was often very hard as well as dangerous.

The quarry cut into half of the mountain with many different large holes and many terraces which formed horizontal 'levels' within each hole, which the quarrymen used to walk along the base and work. Some of the holes were named after where the slate was shipped out to, Australia, California, one was named after a quarry manager, Vivian, some Welsh names such as Twll Mawr (big hole) and one of the bigger features was the Rainbow slab.

The Rainbow slab was a large, dark, sheer face of slate with a wonderful looking ripple, arcing up from the ground on the left, up rightwards to gain the top on the far right. This ripple had first been climbed by John Sylvester who called the route the Rainbow of Recalcitrance. A hard climb. Once the quarry had shut in 1969, climbers had started to develop many of the faces the quarrymen had left. People climbed the routes in pairs, with one person going first and the bottom person feeding out a rope which the top climber clipped through metal protection points, some already in the rock, and some which the 'lead' climber would have to put in. On the Rainbow Slab the climbs were notorious for being bold and many climbers had taken 60-foot falls, with at least one hitting the ground and dying. A serious place to climb with potentially lethal consequences for errors.

When Eleri was younger and had gone on walks with her family, they'd stayed strictly to the paths, whereas as the school years wore on with Lewis, Osian and some of her other friends, they began to explore the holes and levels as far and deep as it was possible to do so. The 3 of them had once found a mannequin in a skip in Dinorwic, carried it to the top of Rainbow slab and threw it over the top as a joke sacrifice. They were hoping to get a response from the security guards in the power station, who had been known to chase climbers off sometimes, but nobody clocked them.

There was often a pool of water, about 60 metres wide and very variable in its depth, in an area known as Dali's Hole.

Sometimes it had no water in at all and had a small forest of skeleton-like dead trees sticking up from its slate-covered base.

It was very near the main walking right of way and it had a slate tower 25 feet high, which braver kids would sometimes jump in off when the depth was deemed suitable. On one occasion, Eleri had jumped in off this to rescue Jordan, who had joined some of their quarry explorations, but who couldn't swim well, if at all. She'd watched him try to scramble around the tower of slate and lose his footing. "Oh shit," she mouthed. There was a fair crowd of friends around but none of them were in the water at this point.

"AHHGGGG!" Her little brother had screamed, before plunging into the azure water and disappearing from sight. He struggled upwards in a feeble effort at trying to swim. He couldn't. Eleri took her glasses off and jumped into the air feet first, black hair flowing upwards as she descended, and landing just to the side of where Jordan was splashing about in a panic. When Eleri re-emerged from her landing, she quickly swam out to him and dragged him to the shallows where they both scampered out, Jordan teary.

Eleri patted him on the back: "You survived Jordan! We'll have to get you practiced at swimming without armbands, or teach you how to climb and scramble well."

Jordan perked up: "Thanks Eleri, don't tell mum."

Eleri: "We definitely won't be telling mum about this, I'll be to blame!"

Zoe had a big grin looking down on them from high above.

Zoe: "Nice one Eleri, I thought we were going to lose our little mascot then."

Lewis had jumped in too, but was too slow to help. Osian, never a water baby, looked down with his thick glasses. His sight was worse than Eleri's and he looked slightly put out he'd not been able to help.

When they got back up to the top, Osian got his camera out and took a picture of Jordan getting held between Eleri and Zoe, each with an arm around him grinning with mirth, and Jordan with an 'I'm-glad-to-be-alive-smile' look. A few days later, Osian gave Eleri a black and white of the picture he'd got developed, which would make her smile to look at, even years later.

Eleri had gotten into climbing with a rope, having joined Lewis on some easier climbs to build knowledge and confidence in the skills necessary. She'd soon surpassed Lewis in terms of ability and Lewis would generally let Eleri go first on climbs to show the way. She was proud to have done one of the climbs on the Rainbow slab, a route called 'Pull my Daisy'. Lewis and Osian both struggled to come up behind her, with her safeguarding them with a rope above them.

The slate quarries were perhaps her favourite place to climb. The climbing was easy angled, usually quite a bit less than vertical, what climbers called slab climbing. The holds were in-cut, and the style required good balance, flexibility and confidence, but was rarely as strenuous as routes found on steeper rock types, like limestone. This particular area also had a fantastic view of the Llanberis pass and the 'peppermint tower', where the end scene of Willow had been made, the film they'd been so into as kids.

As a climber, there was also an amazing film she told her friends to see, whether or not they were into climbing, called 'The Quarryman'. The climbing film by Al Hughes had the outrageous climber, Jonny Dawes, climbing a Blank Groove in Twll Mawr. It really was something to watch, and Eleri liked the soundtrack.

On seconding Eleri on the climb called Pull my daisy Osian shouted up: "This is fucking desperate, good effort Eleri!" He shouted up as he struggled to get purchase on the tiny slate footholds. Lewis stayed quiet, concentrating all his energy into not falling.

When they got up next to Eleri, they give her a pat on the shoulder and nod for getting them both up the climb. Nearby, some goats manoeuvred about on the slate piles above some of the climbs, sending the odd bit over the edge, clattering down the 100+ feet to a crash below.

Osian: "They all live in the pumphouse nowadays. My dad said he went to a rave there years ago."

Eleri: "What's the pumphouse?"

Osian: "It's just up there in the trees, let's go for a look."

They walked diagonally across a slate heap, over a fence and, hidden in the woods, Eleri soon noticed a large building, or perhaps three buildings attached. Going to a large opening in the biggest building, with '1948'inscribed in iron above the entrance, they peered in. It had all sorts of large old machinery, a huge transformer, some kind of pumps, and things Eleri had no idea about. They walked inside and all three of them suddenly noticed the powerful smell. Looking down at what they were stood on, they blocked their noses at the same time.

Eleri: "Who would have a rave in a load of goat shit?"

Osian: "It wasn't always like this!"

Lewis, finding a solution to the problem, quickly built and lit a spliff and passed it between them as they explored. The next room was smaller, but with no machinery, and the third room had lots of old machinery in again. Leaving the dark, smelly rooms and heading into the fresh air was a relief, and Eleri doubted she'd be daft enough to go back into that vile environment again. They walked down to the base of the climb they'd done earlier to collect their trainers and spare clothes, and headed back to Bus Stop Quarry where Osian's first car, a small fiesta, awaited them and he dropped them home.

As they drove back into town they saw Mushroom Bob, with his long, shaggy grey hair, throwing a sheep out of his garden. Bob was renowned around the area as being very keen on magic mushrooms; he and his friends collected as many as they could in September and made powerful wine to see them through the rest of the year. He had a fair-sized garden and absolutely hated sheep and farmers by all accounts. There were often a few 'hippy'-looking people floating around his abode, with many locals nicknaming his house the 'Centre for Psychedelics'.

Watching him heave the sheep out, verifying what they'd heard on the grapevine, made them all giggle. Rumour had it that Bob's partner Beth had had a fight with one of the swans on Llyn Padarn once. Once of the swans had started to peck her old dog quite aggressively and she'd grabbed its long neck with both hands and swung it round and round before slinging it as far as she could into the lake. All parties survived by all accounts. Eleri could never look at a swan without thinking about it being catapulted by Beth.

On another visit into the quarries with Zoe and Isabelle, they explored the outskirts of the huge pits of Twll Mawr and the connecting holes, Mordor and Lost World. These holes were the deepest in the quarries in terms of vertical height, at perhaps 400 feet deep. It was possible to gain the base of Mordor and Lost World via 'scary' ladders the quarrymen had left in place. In the lower parts of the holes were luminous mosses and lichens and all sorts of strange vegetation. Throwing rocks from the top and listening to the 'pang' when they hit the bottom, Eleri announced to her friends:

"These are about 400 feet deep here! If I murdered either of you, I'd hide your bodies in the bottom, nobody would find you there!"

Zoe and Isabelle chuckled at this. The first set of ladders led down just 40 feet, to a gap between Twll Mawr and Mordor, known as the Khyber pass. Two more steep ladders led down into the lower realms of Mordor. The ladders stood a meter out from the rock, and flexed a bit as the girls' weight moved up and down them. The odd missing rung of a ladder gave pause for thought, as though one might come off when either of them was pulling on it.

Eleri was very relaxed and arrived at the lower level first. Zoe and Isabelle eventually joined her, excited and out of breath. Surrounded by huge vertical slate walls, they made their way along a flat terrace to a small tunnel.

Eleri: "This leads through to Lost World."

Moving carefully through the tunnel so as not to bang their heads on the roof, the light at the end led the way. When they looked out at the end, Isabelle said what they were all thinking:

"Wow, so cool."

There was a huge vertical slate wall to their right, covered in a strange orangey red lichen, making it seem like something from Mars. This had the odd tunnel poking out into the void 100 foot or more up the sheer wall. Off to the left were more sheer walls, but these were more the usual slate grey. The base of the deep hole where they were stood had some chest-high trees and plants, and a small slate house, which looked like it must have been placed there by a tornado like in the Wizard of Oz.

They headed towards this, and going into the dark interior, Eleri and Zoe sparked their lighters up to offer some illumination. It looked pretty basic to Eleri; a flat slate floor, a small chimney, long tree logs laid across the roof, which then had big flat slates laid on them. A fairly standard quarry hut.

Then she heard Isabelle yell right next to her ear!

"Shit, you two, stop your lighters!"

Eleri and Zoe: "Why!?"

Isabelle: "There's some fucking powdwr du (gunpowder) over

there! It says it on top of the metal box."

Zoe and Eleri put their lighters away, both breathing out deeply. After a good few seconds their eyes adjusted enough to see the large box Isabelle had spotted.

Eleri: "Give me a hand with this Zoe!"

Breathing hard, they grappled with the oblong box, a metre long and half a metre wide.

Isabelle: "I don't know what you two are doing, this is absolutely daft!"

Zoe prized open the top of the box, providing a view of about 2 dozen grey rubber bags.

"It looks dry!" Zoe exclaimed.

Isabelle stood well back. "You two are absolutely dense! What if it goes off!? You'll blow us all up!"

Eleri: "It's not going to go off unless we light it. Let's just take one bag and put the rest back inside."

Once the box was back in the small house, Eleri opened the bag on a large flat slate boulder and poured out a few inches of the black powder into a line on the slate. She took the rest of the rubber bag into the house and, coming out, went towards the slate.

Eleri: "Let's see if it still works!"

Zoe laughed.

Isabelle: "Don't be stupid Eleri." Rushing to hide behind some large blocks 50 metres away. Eleri snaked the line of powder so a very thin line came towards her, leading to a larger pile a few feet away. Crouching with most of her body below the large slate, she took out her lighter and lit the pile.

SHWOOOOOSH. The blast went a couple of metres into the air

Zoe: "Fuck! Eleri are you ok?"

She peered from where she'd been hiding 10 metres away and when she neared Eleri and saw her through the smoke, she started to laugh.

Zoe: "You've singed your arm and your hair!"

When it became clear the danger was over, Isabelle scampered across to them, shaking her head.

Isabelle: "You mad dickhead, are you ok? I can't believe you did that!"

Eleri: "It works then! Don't tell anyone what I did." With slightly singed hair and a sore hand, she looked at the blast she'd made with such a small amount. Going back inside the slate house, she put moss over the powder box to hide it.

Eleri: "I think it's time to go."

Isabelle: "You can say that again! I can't believe you, you nut case."

Glad to still be alive, they made their way back through the tunnel and out up the ladders, giggling at Eleri's antics. Eleri was feeling glad her arm didn't hurt too much to hold onto the ladder rungs.

Ravens circled high in the holes and cawed as they made their way out, beady black eyes curious.

A week or two later Isabelle came around Eleri's house and handed her a drawing she had made, which made Eleri laugh in delight when she saw it. It had the house made of slate, climbers going up a slab way behind, one of whom you could clearly see was supposed to be Osian with his big glasses sticking out from his face. Near the slate house was an explosion mid-blast, two girls hiding a bit away, and Eleri drawn in with a mixture of fear and surprise, with a mischievous grin on her face, cowering under a rock right next to the blast. There were ravens circling above.

Eleri: "This is outstanding Isabelle! it must have taken you ages to do."

Isabelle: "Although it was a demented experience, I thought it deserved commemorating in some way. After all, we survived! I know you love the slate quarries too. It's an atmospheric place, especially when it feels like a war zone!"

Eleri: "I haven't got anything I can give you except my gratitude, obviously," she said as she put it up next to the other drawing Isabelle had given her of the Morrigan.

Megan came in through the door and looked at the drawing on the wall. "Ha, so that's what went on when you scorched your eyebrows! You're lucky mum didn't twig. How you doing Isabelle? You are an awesome artist you know."

Isabelle: "Thanks a lot Megan. I'm good thanks, how about you? Been busy?"

Megan: "Started work in the old folks' home in Bangor. Lots of nightshifts, super tired all the time."

Isabelle: "I bet, mum did some for a few months once and had to sleep loads during the day. She wasn't herself either, quite ratty. I stepped lightly around her after a shift. She'd always tell me 'I'm just going to have 40 winks' then was out for a few hours middle of the day."

Megan: "It's funny you've got the quarries in there - some of the people in the home used to work in there before it closed. They've got some cool stories to tell, sounds pretty dodge mind."

Eleri: "Dodgy doesn't come into it, look how many quarrymen died or were maimed while the quarries were working. Not including the ones with long term injuries and ailments, that's what got our grandad and his dad."

Isabelle: "I'm sorry about them. Just avoid setting off any more explosions there or else you'll be experiencing a similar level of danger, I'm sure!"

Megan: "If you do it again, I'll tell mum!"

Eleri: "You both sound like my mum. Anyway, like she always tells us, we've got roots in the quarries. Spiritual roots."

Isabelle and Megan both raised their eyebrows at this statement, but Eleri felt a strong connection with the quarries. It used to be the heartbeat of the local communities, with so many lives tethered to them. She had a great deal of fond memories already from exploring the places there, and had risked her life a few times in some of these explorations. The Welsh word 'Hiraeth' was what Eleri felt for the quarries, a longing for and deep connection with the land.

CHAPTER 4:
GWAITH (WORK)

There was no two ways about it, a great deal of work was absolutely shit. Eleri had heard her parents and Megan moan about the jobs they were doing on more than one occasion.

Gwawr: "The queue out of Pete's Eats was endless. I didn't have a break all day and the cook was hungover to sin, so lots of people were complaining about how slow the food was going out and they didn't get what they asked for."

Ray: "He's a bellend of a manager; small minded, jealous, and bullies people. He doesn't care about staff welfare at all, just the bottom line."

Megan: "Nightshifts at the old folks' home are so tiring, I feel wrecked on my days off."

Eleri doubted it was as duff as school at the time she heard some of these mutters, but once Megan had started to work as a waitress in a local pub, she also warned Eleri:

"Pissed people can be a nightmare to deal with. Some of the gits try and grab my arse and others get aggy over sod all." It made Eleri think back to Miss Smith's warning about drunk drivers.

*

Eleri's first experience of work was working in a small local cafe in the middle of Llanberis, Caffi Mafon, on Saturdays with Zoe.

They were in at 9.00 to clean up and then opened at 9.30. The proprietor, Leah, was a very relaxed boss and left them to it to serve teas, coffees, cakes and a few quiches and vegan sausage rolls.

It could sometimes feel fraught, as Gwawr had mentioned, with queues out of the door, milk and change running out, and customers not always too understanding. The heat from the oven and steam from the coffee machine could add to the 'hot headed' feeling. Having Zoe there made it a lot less stressful at busy times; she'd just give a big grin when things got stressful.

When it was quiet, it was cool to see her friends who popped by, but she found it stressful if they came when it was busy. She also hated it when any 'poshos' came and looked down their noses at her. Georgina Booth was the worst, as if she'd ever have to do any normal work in her life. Her parents were loaded and she seemed to treat a lot of people like shit.

One of the days she walked in wearing a blue Gucci dress with sequins on the upper half. It did look stylish to be fair, but more than a bit out of place in Llanberis.

Georgina: "Working here Eleri? Better than cleaning toilets I suppose." She sniggered to her friend Briony, who was similarly dolled up.

Eleri never had warmed to Georgina, ever since her time in lower school where she'd given Matthew a hard time. If, at this point, there was someone in the world she disliked most, it would be Georgina. Since she'd challenged Georgina years before about bullying, she'd always put on an imperious air, and would try to put Eleri and her friends down, given the opportunity. She clearly still believed in a class system and Eleri was bottom of the rung, a servant perhaps.

Her parents used to drop her off in school in a snazzy new BMW or Land Rover, and as soon as she could learn to drive, they got her an Audi A3. She bragged that they were going to buy her a house in Cambridge for when she started university there. Eleri doubted that Georgina would ever have to knuckle down to any actual work unless she chose to, and as she had her aspirations in the banking sector, she expected to get paid a shit ton for any hours worked.

Eleri didn't think that there were good or bad people, as some commentators made out, only good deeds and bad deeds, with any person being open to do either if the environment and circumstances were just right. But Georgina did test the water of this philosophy.

To Eleri, Georgina and her kindred spirits inhabited a completely different planet. Many were doing volunteer work in organisations "to get experience", but who could afford to work for nothing? They seemed to float through life without a care, or so it seemed to Eleri.

Georgina continued to insult Eleri and Zoe for a minute, almost unconsciously before demanding two cappuccinos.

Eleri and Zoe looked at each other, eyebrows raising, both tapping into their inner bastards. Eleri's mind wondered what she could spike Georgina's coffee with. Zoe had obviously read Eleri's mind and, turning around with a smirk on her face to make the coffees, she dropped laxatives that the manager had left in the kitchen area into both brews. It was some days later when Georgina gave Eleri one of the most evil stares she'd ever received, that Eleri realised Zoe's spiking had delivered the karma they had been looking for.

*

After they'd shut up at 4.30pm and cleaned, they'd usually go down to Llyn Padarn for a smoke if the weather was nice. It was always a sense of relief when they closed up.

She got about £20 for the day.

On one summer's day after work, they made the mistake of getting in the car with a guy called Jonny Dawes,a very famous climber and the main 'hero' in the climbing film Eleri liked, called 'The Quarryman'. Eleri hadn't heard about his driving though. He pulled up next to them in Llanberis high street in a green Seat, which had a loud exhaust.

Jonny asked: "You two fancy going for a swim down at Llyn Gwynant? I'm going to go there for a change."

Zoe spoke for both of them: "Ace, free ride." Eleri got in the back and Zoe the front.

Jonny grinned: "Slow, medium or fast?"

Zoe: "Fast, obviously."

As they left Llanberis, suddenly Eleri's face went backwards as the car shot forwards a lot faster than she would have imagined. Zoe screamed with delight, and Eleri just said, "fucking hell" when she'd recovered from the shock. As they went around the first bend, the exhaust hit the ground, sending sparks behind them. Only a mile out of town, Eleri felt she'd used up all her adrenaline. Her stomach was full of butterflies, but she didn't feel like being the party pooper by telling him to slowdown. Overtaking everything on the road on the way up the Llanberis Pass, and often squeezing in between other cars with an inch or two to spare, Eleri thought that Jonny was a very good driver, very lucky and a bit dense at the same time. She'd not seen the like in movies even.

Stepping out of the car at the edge of Llyn Gwynant, Eleri brushed sweat from her forehead, and re-adjusted her glasses higher up her nose before telling Jonny:

"Thanks a lot for the ride, I think we'll hitch back though!"

Jonny looked disappointed.

Eleri and Megan laughed as they watched the sparks fly as he took off around the first bend like a rocket. They chatted about feeling lucky to be alive.

*

Her next experience of work was working in a shop in Bangor which sold outdoors gear, The Great Arete. She worked Saturdays but also some weekdays during school holidays, and for slightly better pay - £35. As she got the bus into Bangor, she didn't have to pay, as Thomas let her off, although it did mean he expected her to chat with him for the duration there and back. She nicked rollies off him, figuring she was doing him a favour, with the possibility that it reduced the amount he smoked.

The shop had clothes and equipment for walking and climbing; waterproofs, stoves, climbing shoes, harnesses, ropes. The manager, Steve, was a nice enough guy in his mid-40s, with dark, greying hair. He spent a lot of his time looking at stock lists and things to buy, as well as working out good deals to give students who would come into the shop after they'd received their student loans and spend it all.

Eleri liked climbing herself but found it quite intimidating chatting to people about what to buy, or the differences between things. And when she started to do a few days a week, she found it desperately boring, often waiting for hours for anyone to come into the shop. Inevitably, people would come in just before they were about to shut, which meant they stayed open late. To Eleri, the hours felt like a prison sentence, and although Steve was a nice enough guy, he wasn't very talkative.

He also played the same CD again and again and again - Blood on the tracks by Bob Dylan. It was an album Eleri appreciated, but had quite enough of by the end, and she was forced to make Steve's favourite CD disappear. It sounded like the owner of the shop didn't pay Steve much for managing it, and she felt a little sorry for him; he had a partner and two young kids to look after, and he seemed to work pretty long hours. He was quietly spoken and had a very calm demeanour.

Eleri: "How long have you worked here?"

Steve: "Ten years. That's a lot of my 30s spent in here. Dolly Parton was right about working 9 to 5!"

Eleri: "Has your salary gone up much over that time to keep you here?"

Steve: "No, I did ask Glyn who owns it for a pay rise once, but he wasn't keen and there didn't seem to be many other job options for me to move into. It can feel harder when you get older to have the confidence to go for new stuff. You won't know about that kind of doubt at your age, at least I hope not. I've got kids to look after too so I don't want to rock the boat."

Eleri: "If you've committed that much time to a business, I think you deserve some reward though. I'd start another conversation with Glyn."

Steve shrugged: "Maybe," sounding like he wouldn't. Eleri had seen the figures going through when the accountant was in. Glyn made quite a bit from the shop and could easily give Steve a bit more money.

Steve: "I started nursing for a few years, but found the nightshifts murder, ended up depressed. This feels a lot better for my wellbeing by comparison. You've got to see it in a positive light, same as anywhere you go to regularly. A few friends who work in an office say it feels like going to prison every day they are there, and some of them have been in the same place for twenty years or more!"

Eleri nodded with sympathy.

*

In Bangor, Eleri got to know a couple who were homeless and would usually sleep in or around the high street, with the park near the cathedral being a common haunt. In the rural communities there never seemed to be anyone 'living rough', at least none that Eleri had clocked. Mark and Karen had been seeing each other for a year and were on a list with the council to get into some social housing towards Dickies Boat Yard, but they were in a reasonable sized queue apparently.

Mark had long brown hair and a long beard and moustache and must have been about six foot. Karen was tiny by comparison, with long dark hair tied in a ponytail. She always had on the same pretty yellow dress with different birds pictured all over it. Both were in their early 40s, had slightly sun-weathered faces and often sported large rucksacks with their sleeping gear and extra clothes in. They'd met whilst sleeping in the same area of one of the parks in Bangor one night and had clicked straight away. Eleri liked that they'd found love whilst in a precarious place in life.

They got food out of the supermarket bins which had been chucked because of the sell by date, and they sometimes helped out when some of the shops needed a load of stuff lifted and moved into vans and got a tiny bit of money.

Eleri chatted to them in her breaks when they were around and had bought them fish and chips a few times. It seemed they'd hit a few branches of unluckiness in life. Both had no family. Mark's partner had left him and then he got made redundant from his job in a sugar factory in Bury St Edmunds and struggled to afford rent. He got his few belongings and train-hopped to North Wales, leaving the memories in that town behind him.

Karen didn't want to chat about her past but seemed to be happy enough; all they seemed to need was each other. Eleri did feel relief when they finally got into some accommodation just before winter really kicked in. She didn't know how homeless people managed when it got truly arctic, and she knew she'd be awake in her own bed thinking about them if they'd not gotten sorted. It made her wonder back to Matthew Vasquez and how he was getting on. She was fairly certain when they were younger he spent a lot of time out on the streets rather than in a bed.

Occasionally sales representatives would come into the shop to chat about some wares and, better still, give Eleri and Steve some free stuff. Ben Bransby, a fairly famous climber, had come into the shop once to chat about DMM gear. Eleri couldn't believe how small he was. Wearing thick glasses, he reminded her of Penfold from Danger Mouse. There was a poster of him on the wall of the shop on a very high boulder called Cornelius. Eleri had tried to start a conversation with him but his replies were so monosyllabic that Eleri had to do most of the talking.

*

It was not far to Osian's house from the shop, only around a mile, and she enjoyed popping over to his after work where Elliw, Osian's mum, would ply her with lovely food and slag off Glyn and Osian for making a mess before Eleri could see what projects Osian would be working on.

Elliw: "They've taken over half my writing shed with all their mess now. Osian's in there more than Glyn too!"

When Eleri arrived one day, she saw bright flashes and sparks streaming out of the work shed. Creeping up to see, she watched Osian welding what looked like a strange chair.

Eleri: "What are you working on here Osian, you aren't making an electric chair to fry Lewis in?"

Osian: "Hi Eleri, good day at work? I'm trying to make a wheelchair that's comfy and lightweight and will fit my cousin, Jude. She's got one that she uses, but it's pretty shit and uncomfortable. I'm trying to make this one a bit more curvy and more manoeuvrable. I'll give it thicker tyres so it can be good for going across fields and more 'off-piste' than some of the standard ones."

Eleri was impressed with Osian's ingenuity, hard work and skill.

Eleri: "Fucking good effort Osian, I wouldn't know where to start! When will it be ready do you think? You could make more than one, there may be lots of people who could do with a wheelchair like this."

Osian: "It will be another month before I've got it ready to test and play around. You could help me with that, should be a laugh! Could do a tour of some of the fields near here."

Eleri: "Sounds like a great plan to me, I can't wait to see it working."

Every time Eleri left Osian's house, she always felt that he was someone who was fortunate to have found a love for making things early on in life and had developed incredible skills and creativity. Many of their other friends spent most of their time getting baked, although Lewis did a bit of climbing and reading when not getting stoned.

Some of her friends had said they had gotten up for work having gone to big parties the night before. They'd still been drunk the next morning and not realised it, leading to some very near misses. One guy from school, Mark Leaves, had wrapped his van around a corner one night, on the outskirts of Cwm-Y-Glo. The van was a write-off but luckily Mark got away with it pretty unscathed. He still lost his license and wouldn't be getting it back anytime soon. It had been a nice van too.

*

Her sister had started to work at a retirement home when she turned 18 and seemed to spend all her time working nightshifts. She developed dark 'bags' under the eyes after a bit of time doing the work that contrasted sharply to her pale skin and blonde hair. Eleri's conversations with Megan made her think this line of work could be very hard.

Megan: "Mr Jones has Alzheimer's and often forgets where he is. He'll start walking around the place at three in the morning and we have to get him back to his room. He can be pretty hard work. His family come to visit him sometimes, but he can hardly remember who they are. There is often a lot of mess to clean up after some of them too, poor dears."

Eleri: "I hope I don't live to get Alzheimer's."

Megan: "It's definitely not a nice thing to get. Getting old is hard enough as it is. I'm definitely going to try and quit smoking too; three of the people here are only in their 60s and are on oxygen. I think they've got Emphysema and it looks grim."

Eleri: "We should both give up. It's a great effort what you're doing, looking after the golden oldies."

Megan: "Thanks sis. It looks quite lonely for some of them, the ones who don't have families."

Eleri: "I hope I don't get old. You're not selling it!"

Megan: "We all get old eventually Eleri, and you want a family around you when you do."

One day when she was in Bangor and hanging out having lunch on a bench near the High Street, Eleri met a cleaner who was also taking lunch on the same bench. Amiria worked in the Bangor University Halls and was from Papua New Guinea originally. She said she also worked in a retirement home nearby and she was shocked at how older people were treated here.

In Papua New Guinea she said older family members were very respected and looked after within the family, whereas here they were given away to strangers to be looked after, and left to be very lonely and forgotten about. She couldn't believe it.

Amiria: "How can you treat your older family members that way?" She asked Eleri, not accusingly, but with a level of anguish in the question, that she saw a great wrong in the world and was horrified by it.

Eleri blushed, it wasn't something she'd ever given any thought.

Eleri: "I'm sorry it's not very nice how we do some things over here. Not all older people are treated like this. I guess our society has become too much about individualism and we can forget about the really important things in life."

Eleri felt very embarrassed about how shit it seemed to be and wondered what her, Megan and Jordan would do with Gwawr and Ray when they were old. Between the three of them she was sure they could look after them and probably look after Thomas too.

*

Her brother Jordan's first line of work also looked grim to Eleri. He left school at 16 and started labouring for a couple of builders in the area. Mixing cement, heaving rocks out of piles of mud all day, and sometimes digging drainage trenches in the rain and the cold. Although her work in the shop had been boring as hell, at least it lacked the brutality of Jordan's work. He came in from work piss wet through, with cement dust and mud all over his clothes. It looked desperate to get clean. He always looked haggard and, after half a bottle of wine, would go to bed dead early. He also seemed to always have a minor injury; cuts from saws, lime in his eye which took days for his inflamed eye to go down, and tons of near misses he'd chat through, from getting blown across a room having cut through a live wire which was meant to be dead, to scaffolding collapsing which had been rearranged in a dodgy manner. His mate Paddy, who he often worked with, was sound at least, but Eleri didn't think it would be a great long-term career option. Eleri remembered one grim job he was chatting about.

Paddy: "I was working in a dark cellar in Clwt-y-Bont, super damp and cold, and Tim who was running the job was having a funny one, in a pretty bad mood most of the time. We were having endless rollie breaks and I only put in for pay for the hours that I was doing, which wasn't very many so I made bugger all each day. Then Tim got his ribs kicked in outside the pub one night. It was pretty bad; he broke some. All the electricity was meant to be off in the house, but when I was sawing through some wood in the ceiling, I went through a live wire and it blew me halfway across the room. Then it felt pretty dark on this job, both of us pretty down and miserable. I was well glad when it was over."

Eleri liked to chat to Jordan and make sure he was doing ok. Megan, being a bit older and less into explorations when they were younger, didn't have quite the same connection with him.

Eleri eventually started to take Jordan out climbing, teaching him the basics and suggesting he get into instructing rather than labouring, as from what she'd seen from outdoor instructors, it looked considerably easier than labouring.

Jordan took her up on her advice and soon got a job as a trainee instructor at a local outdoor centre, right on the edge of the slate quarries, Blue Peris. He seemed a lot happier doing this and he was given a room in the centre itself which got him out of the way of Gwawr and Ray. Eleri was chuffed for him. Having looked generally unhappy throughout much of school, it would have been bleak for his work life to have panned out in a similar vein.

*

Eleri soon came to realise that work wasn't too different from school. Working hard could pay off, friendly people seemed to do well, and bosses varied from ace, knowledgeable and supportive to clueless, overpaid arseholes. She also noticed that arguments were often caused by one or more people suffering from lack of sleep, or something a bit grim which had occurred in their life recently. She realised that people from relatively wealthy backgrounds would normally filter into 'professional' jobs, and people from her background would struggle. The difference in wealth of a poorer working-class family and a middle-class family will often be hundreds of times difference and could be quite a game changer in life chances. When you are from the poorer end, she noticed that it is easy to become 'aspiration-less'.

At around the time of getting into more regular work, Gwawr was adamant that Eleri needed to learn to drive.

Gwawr: "It's essential for work in rural areas. I know Ray gets away without it but that's because I run him about a lot of the time. You know what the buses are like around here."

Eleri wasn't that psyched at first and she had a few minor rows with Gwawr who, to be fair, it must have been pretty stressful for. When Eleri put her foot on the breaks it felt that it took the car forever to actually slow down and come to a stop.

"Ahhhh!!" screamed Gwawr when Eleri went off the road, taking a corner in fourth gear when she should have been in second. They went over a curb and the car plonked onto a piece of grass.

Eleri: "Sorry mum." She hopped out of the car stressed as sin and refused to get back in.

Gwawr was adamant that Eleri could sort it out and, after some persuasion, Eleri got the car back on the road and continued on towards their house, driving slowly. As she grew more experienced behind the wheel, it made her realise how insane Jonny's driving had been the day he'd taken her and Zoe for a spin. She passed her driving test on her second attempt with much relief, as more driving lessons would have cost her plenty more days work in the shop and more stress for Gwawr.

*

Eleri had gotten a taste of various types of work but still had it in mind to find work related to the teachings of her favourite teacher. She knew for this she'd have to continue to keep her head down with studies and find out about which organisations looked most appealing to aim towards.

*

Elsewhere in Britain, at a similar time, were people that Eleri had speculated on, who would do little work, other than heckling each other, and whose wealth would allow them to go into jobs that they very clearly didn't have the competence to do.

"Oink, oink, oink." They debated, lied and bullied their way upwards, trampling over any 'ordinary little people' as they went. "Oink!"

CHAPTER 5:
CARIAD (LOVE)

By the time Eleri was into her late 20s she'd had a few different relationships. There were a fair few brief ones when she was younger, one longer term one for seven years or so with Jacob Jones, and one long term 'simmering' possibility that fate had never consummated.

Eleri had read some research that looked at couples who had separated and those which had lasted some time. They asked the people in relationships a simple question.

"Is love a choice or a feeling?"

Those who split generally said love was a feeling; those that lasted said love was a choice. It made perfect sense to Eleri, but she also wondered at what point someone should throw in the towel if things change a lot. After all, people can change considerably. On a sliding scale with a perfect partner at one end, to someone who becomes a nutcase and tries to murder you and your relatives at the other, at some point along that scale, surely every person has a breaking point. Not that she'd made it to the extreme end of this sliding scale.

She'd loved Jacob for a few years. In the first year of university, she'd clocked him in her Economics module. Five foot ten, dark brown hair and eyes to match, and smart. Very smart. She liked watching him in class, her heart beating a bit faster and her breath quickening when he was in the same room, but she never had the nerve to go up and start a conversation.

The lecturer, Clive, would often trawl out the same story again and again: "If there was a $100 note on the ground, it wouldn't be worth Bill Gates' time to bend down and pick the note up."

Eleri was convinced he'd smoked too much weed in his time.

Although Eleri didn't feel confident enough to approach him during lectures, luckily for her, Jacob was found one winter's night in the huge catacomb bunker on the outskirts of Llanberis, where various raves had been organised over the years. The complex had been built to hold munitions during World War Two and was sturdy enough to prevent the local town of Llanberis being blown to bits had there been any accidents. It was for that reason it was good for keeping very loud beats inside.

To access it required a small detour out of town and a scramble down the only accessible side which led to a large, concrete football-pitch-sized oblong, with 20-foot vertical concrete walls on three sides and a large doorway on one of these walls which led into the huge bunker. Eleri had heard some guy called Jerry had organised this particular night.

She'd gone down with a fair team of friends after having a few drinks in the Heights, the largest pub in Llanberis. Lewis, Osian, Zoe, Isabelle, and some friends she'd met from Sheffield had come over, Lizzy, Liz and Bob. Liz and Bob were the ultimate raver couple, always at big parties, and they seemed to manage it well without becoming zombies. They were also great company for going full tilt. Lizzy was a great dancer and a dab hand with vertical dancing on ribbons.

Lewis seemed to be pretty well-connected and had sorted them out with a few pills and a bag of MDMA. To be fair, most young people in the area Eleri knew seemed to have a large supply of pills, ket, acid and coke so she wasn't concerned about having a shortage. When they were scrambling down to the rave with several other random people she didn't know, they could hear the whirring of the generator, but no music.

Eleri had heard about this venue but had never been. It seemed nuts. Passing the people smoking outside, they headed through the large doorway. A pathway led inside for a hundred metres with disgusting deep water running alongside it. Apparently an unfortunate party-goer had fallen into this earlier. It looked highly unappealing and if anyone was ever doing risk assessments for events like these, the minging-looking water, which very screwed people could definitely drown in, would be high on the list of hazards.

Where the pathway ended, stairs led upwards, and they began to hear music. Doubling back on themselves at the top of the stairs, the music became pounding and rhythmic and they entered along room with lots of people at the far end and a multitude of coloured lasers flashing through the haze. The music was powerful enough to make it feel that Eleri's chest was moving.

"Jesus," Osian let out with a huge grin.

Marshalling at the quieter end of the 'dance room', they put some of their bags and rucksacks against the side walls.

Eleri, Zoe and Isabelle got out the bag of MDMA and, each licking their little fingers, had a dip or two and a lick, then washed the slightly unnatural taste down with some San Miguel. Lewis stepped over and offered them a big green pill. Isabelle shook her head, but when Eleri looked to Zoe, she grinned before they halved it. Eleri's stomach did turns in the anticipation of the drugs kicking in. They were ready.

Boom, boom, boom, boom, boom, boom.

Making their way forward, the lasers bounced off lots of faces, some of whom Eleri knew, at least vaguely, and a few she didn't.

Eleri, Zoe and Isabelle moved from dancing in a huddle, and dancing in a line, their hands in the air and grins on their faces, with Osian and the rest of the crew nearby, hands pounding the air.

When the drugs started to kick in for Eleri, the music became louder, more rhythmic, and a powerfully warm feeling and energy enveloped her whole body. Her pupils dilated, eyes fully black, leaving no room for their usual colour, almost like how people appear when they look at someone they are in love with. She made her way to the front where she could see the DJ. Her friends were right behind her.

Eleri's sister Megan had never done drugs, although she liked a G&T. Eleri thought she was really missing out on a powerful experience. She saw Jordan at some point and went to make sure he was ok, but he seemed to be having a great night too.

She knew the woman who was DJing, Rosie, who was absolutely loving it. Eleri and team got their hands in the air and were spinning round, high as kites. It seemed that the whole of North Wales was in there partying; this was the community at its best.

Between hands in the air and grinding against Zoe and Isabelle, Eleri eventually clocked the guy in the dark shirt, also near the front, dancing like hell. Jacob. She had chatted to Zoe and Isabelle about him, and they both nodded. Eleri needed nothing more. Inhibitions truly gone; the lack of nerve no longer mattered. She made her move.

Moving in front of him, her back to his front, she started to dance nearer. When his hands touched her side, she turned her head and nodded, moving back into him more. His grip strengthened and they started to get down, Eleri kissing him backwards. They danced together for hours until the final tunes.

"Music is made to make you move, music is made to make you move..." until the generator eventually ran out of petrol. Moving slowly out of the bunker into daylight, they stood outside for a minute, wrapped in each other's arms. The drugs had started to wear off a little, but, with pupils still highly dilated, they shared a rollie. Zoe and Isabelle had moved outside and, after snorting some ket, they also shared a rollie, Zoe smirking at Eleri. Even people who didn't smoke loved smoking when they were on ecstasy.

Eleri: "You coming back to mine?"

Jacob: "I'd love to, where is that?"

Eleri: "It's a 20-minute walk from here, Brynrefail, end of the lake."

Jacob: "Lovely place."

Once out of the concrete depths, the morning was wonderful. Soft golden light streamed through the trees, and they walked in it, following the path next to the lake back to the village. Eleri opened the door to the two bedroom terraced house on the high street that she shared with Zoe, almost opposite Caffi Caban.

Going upstairs and into bed once the drugs had worn off enough, they spent the rest of the day screwing. It was good sex. Most men Eleri had been with loved it when she patted their balls or grasped hard onto their arse, and Jacob wasn't shy of going down on her for some time during one of their sessions on that first day together. They slept a long time when they finally crashed and woke up sometime Monday afternoon, having missed all of their lectures. Eleri made a fire in the woodburning stove in the living room and they cuddled in front of it for the rest of the day, chatting and smoking. Eleri presumed Zoe had gone off to an after party, or was hiding in her room.

Eleri: "Where do you live?"

Jacob: "Near Newborough beach, on Anglesey."

Eleri: "How do you get into lectures? It's a good few miles into uni."

Jacob: "Same way I got to the party, on my bike."

Eleri: "Jesus, good effort!"

"I guess I might be," Jacob said, laughing.

From then on, Jacob spent most of his time at Eleri's house rather than on Anglesey. Luckily Zoe seemed to get on with him.

*

Through university, they studied and supported each other. Jacob was studying economics and maths, whereas Eleri had gotten stuck into politics and international development.

They listened to the Levellers, Verve, Faithless and Massive Attack all the time. Fifteen Years, Urban Hymns, Salva Mea, Unfinished Symphony, Fun Loving Criminals. Nothing particularly new, but plenty of classics which could be enjoyed time and again.

Eleri got on well with his parents, Hilary and George, and enjoyed going around to their house where they would feed them steaks, pizzas, wine, and even the odd reefer. Properly cool parents. Hilary was tall, with shoulder length dark hair and the confidence found in many doctors who make life or death decisions. George was of similar height to Hilary but with stacked shoulders, possibly gained from lugging boats around at Plas Menai, the sailing centre where he worked.

Gwawr and Rays' eyebrows raised when Eleri first brought Jacob round for a meal with them.

Gwawr: "Can you walk to Newborough beach from your house? We used to go out with the kids, it's a lovely spot. What's the name of the little island?"

Jacob: "Llanddwyn. It is very beautiful, me and Eleri have walked out there a few times."

Gwawr: "I hope she's not gotten you into climbing too."

Jacob: "Not going to happen for me, I like to get pictures of her doing it though. I'm not too keen on heights."

Gwawr: "Very wise, me neither! She probably got it off Ray, doing silly things."

Ray: "The talent she got from me for sure."

*

On a walk near Llanberis, they had taken their friend's German Shepherd, Sunny, out for the afternoon. She was small and cute looking, and apparently hated postmen. Jacob let her off the lead on the walk in the fields near Gifach Ddu and the river.

Eleri: "Are you sure she'll be ok with the sheep?"

Jacob: "Yeah, sure she'll be fine."

After about a minute, Sunny shot towards some of the sheep. Eleri and Jacob shouted "Shit!" at the same time and started legging it after the dog. Running towards the river, the sheep dove in and Sunny went after it.

Eleri: "Get in after them Jacob!"

Jacob duly jumped in and before long had a wet sheep which weighed a ton in one hand, and a bedraggled German Shepherd in the other. Eleri burst out laughing at the sight as Jacob struggled to make his way back out, before putting Sunny back on the lead.

*

Eleri continued to apply herself in lectures as she had in secondary school, putting a good deal of energy into studying around them and making detailed lists in her diaries, from things learned to things she needed to do. She'd heard from some of her friends studying psychology that people who have written goals were considerably more likely to achieve them, and that process-based goals were more successful than outcome-based goals. She tried to make the most of these points for preparing for exams and for some of her climbing related goals too.

Some of the lectures tested her patience.

She got particularly peeved off by one lecturer, Dr Hunt. In his late 40s, greying, and wearing a near-permanent frown, he clearly found life a bit sour when he wasn't looking smug about putting people down.

In a room with around 50 students facing him in a small arc, he drawled.

Dr Hunt: "Let's discuss Rhodri Morgan, the First Minister of Wales, and his decision not to introduce choice and competition into public services in Wales. This went against UK Labour Party Policy, and he said it 'did not fit Welsh attitudes and values'. But Tony Blair recently claimed that he was saving Britain's public services with his reform agenda, bringing in some elements of privatisation."

Eleri piped up as soon as he'd finished.

Eleri: "I think Rhodri Morgan will be proved correct in his decisions. Blair is relying on workers from the private sector to make large improvements in the public sector, but it's blue sky thinking. The input from the private is unlikely to be more beneficial. How is a private sector manager going to be better than the current NHS managers we already have? Are they more qualified? The people that are currently in high level roles are not dense. Rhodri Morgan and Welsh Labour have promoted collaboration between public services, rather than competition. It seems like a good idea which is working to me. It is also a poor show from UK Labour when a Tory leader is there challenging them on their assumption that the public sector is lazy and inefficient and that the private sector is fantastic."

Dr Hunt's face darkened, as he clearly didn't like the trajectory the discussion had taken.

Dr Hunt: "Competition and the free market have been shown to increase efficiency the world over. It's the reason the Soviet Union collapsed because they neglected this idea, much as Welsh Labour are doing."

Eleri: "The jury is still very much out about competition and free market economics; this so-called neoliberalism. In the 1960s and early 70s, the poorest 20% of the UK got the most from increases in GDP. But since neoliberalism has taken hold, the millionaires and billionaires have been doing the best whilst the poorest 10% have been getting much poorer, having more debts than savings.

You can also look at the health care system in the United States. It's pretty much the opposite of our NHS, being ludicrously expensive and unavailable to anyone from a slightly poorer background. Rhodri Morgan was right to be opposed to the new 'Foundation Hospitals' and Gordon Brown didn't want them to be financially autonomous.

Regarding the collapse of the Soviet Union, it was a lot more complex than lack of a free market. Many of its republics wanted independence from the Central Government. They were always in political and legal conflicts in the decade leading up to it.

The poverty that ran rife thereafter its collapse, many economists blame on the 'shock therapy' of the immediate trade liberalisation and the large-scale privatisation of previously publicly owned assets. I doubt that Welsh counties such as Powys, Gwynedd and Conwy are likely to want independence from the Welsh Government anytime soon."

Dr Hunt glowered, and Jacob nudged Eleri appreciatively. Eleri sincerely hoped Dr Hunt wouldn't be the one marking any of her exam work. She was glad to stick up for Rhodri Morgan and the Welsh Government. She felt they were making the best possible decisions around most matters about which she felt strongly.

*

They'd often go out to parties on weekends, mostly at Hendre Hall, a night club and event facility out on its own, a mile from Bangor. It was effectively a few large barns, with an outdoor hangout and fire area in the middle of a square complex. It was a brilliant venue. Eleri and Zoe had a fair few after-parties at their house, as the main party would normally end between 2-4am and most friends were still pretty dialled then. Taxis back, cups of tea handed out, wood on the fire and tunes that were slightly more mellow, was a fine recipe indeed. Jacob seemed very into it. He seemed very into Eleri.

Jon: "You seem good together, you two."

Jon organised a lot of the parties in the area. Soon after saying this, Liz gave him a big key of ket to snort, which soon had him on a half hour story rant by the fire before he stumbled home.

It often impressed Eleri how many 'professionals' and other eclectic people you found who took drugs and partied hard. Doctors, Paramedics, Psychiatrists, Hippies, Instructors, Students, Labourers, Teachers. Everyone loved a dance, great pumping music and social scene.

Ben Elton's book, High Society, about the lack of political bottle for legalising drugs, was spot on in Eleri's mind. It was alcohol and tobacco which were killing everyone. If they were serious about a 'war on drugs', they'd legalise all of them and make a bit of tax. It wasn't like most politicians weren't necking most drugs themselves.

Jacob didn't climb but would come out to join Eleri when she did, always keen to support her. He got on well with Osian and Lewis and would take pictures.

After finishing university, Eleri got some research contracts for the Joseph Rowntree Foundation, an independent social change organisation working to solve UK poverty. Her work involved travelling to and spending a good deal of time in parts of London, Manchester, Birmingham and Glasgow.

When Eleri started to work away from home a lot more, the relationship was a bit harder, but for a few more years she felt she was the luckiest woman on earth.

Jacob was generally very supportive. She'd be driving back down the M6 and tiredly on the A55 late on a Friday night, really looking forward to seeing Jacob, eating late with him and cooking a nice meal.

There were times when affairs were an option. People she worked with and liked made suggestions, but Eleri ignored them. It would have been stupid to risk her and Jacob's happiness on a fling. She felt 'all in'.

Whereas Eleri worked researching policies around poverty reduction, Jacob wasn't into using his first-class degree in economics and instead preferred to spend time out gardening. Eleri thought that after putting a lot of effort all the way through school, he hit a bit of a wall for carrying on doing similar work.

Eleri still had Miss Smith's teachings in the back of her mind and thought of the many people who were struggling that she had grown up with. She wanted to help make a difference and kept the poorer souls in mind for motivation, which wasn't hard as her work involved speaking to many families and individuals who were struggling for a variety of reasons, often debt.

*

Eleri and Jacob spent more time apart, mainly because Eleri got to the point where she wanted to spend less time with him, even though he was a great and kind person who was really into her, she had lost some of what she felt in the years when she felt the luckiest person on earth. And Eleri's eyes did wander, and she wondered at times what it might be like to be with someone else.

Jacob had affluent parents but was skint himself. Eleri thought his parents should just give him a bit of money to help him out, as that's what she would have done if she had kids. Going out with someone who was skint all the time became a bit wearing, especially when Eleri's family had no wealth, whereas Jacob's were loaded but didn't support him much.

It was one of the things that made Eleri become a bit ratty with him and lose an element of respect, which is often a key element of relationships that can see its strength severely tested over time. Where they'd rarely argued before, there was an increase in the odd heated discussion. The oxytocin had definitely worn off and, later than with many relationships, it was time to either adapt and change...or split.

*

On one day, just before they were about to go out climbing with Lewis and co, Jacob piped up.

Jacob: "Do you not think climbing is quite a selfish thing to do?"

Eleri took this personally, seeing it as an attack on her and many of her close friends. She felt that the supportive side of Jacob had started to disappear.

Eleri: "Everyone is selfish at the end of the day, Jacob, and climbing does little harm. People who have families and look after them well are deemed as great citizens by society, but often fly everywhere without a thought about climate change and buy a lot of their shit from sweatshops. Are you trying to tell me that climbers are more selfish than these people who are simply having lots of children and living lazily, with often little thought for other people or their impact on the environment?"

Jacob: "You know what I mean, the risk."

Eleri: "Driving is riskier Jacob, and selfishness runs pretty evenly throughout society, although from my observations those with more wealth are normally more selfish with it. Some of the most privileged, loaded people I know seem tight gits to be honest! It's almost comical, they'll end up taking their wealth to the grave with them, like an Egyptian pharaoh."

Jacob: "You've definitely got an issue with anyone who has a bit of money you know."

Eleri: "Well I've got a problem with you too, so people clearly don't have to have any money for me to take issue with them!"

Lewis and the small gang of climbers in the car tried to make themselves small and disappear, as if they couldn't hear, before Eleri got in and headed out with them. Pissed off.

It didn't help that the vehicle Eleri had pumped thousands of pounds into to keep on the road, a blue ford escort, became critical and was stressful for any journey where you couldn't be certain you'd be going to make it.

On a trip just before it became critical, she'd taken Jacob up to Glasgow for the week. It hadn't been a great week. Both her and Jacob had been in their own world of worry, concerning money and their relationship, and neither of them were communicating themselves to the other very well. There were a few slightly awkward conversations, with Eleri suggesting possible opportunities which might improve Jacob's financial situation.

Eleri: "You could take that job with the University; it would give some security and you could afford a car."

Jacob: "I don't want that kind of commitment to be honest. Five days a week doesn't give time to do anything else, like socialising. Nobody is on their death bed wishing they worked more Eleri."

Eleri: "There are some people in life wishing they could afford petrol to get back home though."

Jacob: "Sorry I can't afford petrol money."

Eleri: "It's not a problem, I'm just a bit skint at the moment. And that car might not last too much longer; it's been struggling on hills recently."

Jacob: "We'll make it back fine." He sounded confident.

They didn't.

They made it down to just south of Carlisle and then the escort conked out. Eleri had been watching the temperature gauge going up with some concern, when all of a sudden steam started billowing out of the bonnet, making it hard to see the road. Pulling into the hard shoulder with the hazards on, Eleri stepped out feeling exhausted and pissed off. She made a rollie and began smoking, thinking about options for getting home.

Jacob got out smiling, trying to put a cheery face on the predicament, but Eleri wasn't seeing the funny side. She wasn't a member of the AA and it cost £150 for them to come out and tell her the car was dead. He said he would tow it to the nearest breaker's yard. Her credit card was pretty maxed out. They managed to get a lift off the AA guy to Tebay services a few miles south on the M6.

They hungout, drinking tea, in a rather grimy lorry drivers' café, mainly sitting in silence for a time with Eleri thinking uncharitable thoughts about Jacob. Rummaging in her pockets, she looked at their team resources. They had enough tobacco for one and a half rollies and about ten pounds or so in assorted coins. She'd spent a lot of her money the last few months trying to repair the now completely dead car. She wondered how many people had been screwed over by pumping all their money into screwed vehicles and realised that it was an area she hadn't gone into in her current research. She wasn't keen to be using herself as an example of someone becoming destitute because of it either, although she could always ask her parents for a crash for a month. Not everyone had that luxury.

Eleri told Jacob the money was getting spent on some more tobacco and that they would be hitching home. It felt like it took them forever to leave the services, but eventually some guy called Ned in a transporter took pity on them and gave them a lift right to the Chester services. From here it only took them another two hours of hitching before a lovely hippy-looking woman with long, blonde, greying hair called Pippa took them to the OneStop services at the start of the A5, and from then a short hitch got them to Deiniolen and Eleri's parents house. She hadn't wanted to go to Jacob's parents as she felt any feelings of warmth would be too forced, having had a bit of a crap few months with it seeming to her that Jacob had bounced from one epic to another with his work.

Gwawr opened the door for them.

Gwawr: "So, the escort finally died. You didn't sing its praises the last few times you were here."

Eleri: "We've had a pretty epic journey back, I feel bolloxed."

"You should play it safe and get a Nissan, Japanese made cars last forever," Ray said, chipping in behind Gwawr.

Gwawr gave Ray a dirty look.

Gwawr: "Our Nissan Cherry didn't last forever, did it?"

When it had died, Gwawr and Ray decided against getting another and just to use the bus to get into work. Ray was happy enough with this as he couldn't drive anyway, and it meant more time with Thomas.

After a late-night feast, they crashed out and Jacob got Megan's old bunk.

*

Soon after the breakdown incident, Eleri decided to blow out her relationship with Jacob, which she found incredibly hard and painful as he didn't want to split up. She felt she couldn't change herself enough not to find Jacob's faults too annoying. Jacob had managed to hit Eleri's 'breaking point' on the sliding scale.

Every time Eleri saw an escort on the road after the epics she'd had with hers, she stared daggers at it for the stressful times it had given her. When she had saved enough money again, she took her dad's advice and picked up a cheap purple Almera, which seemed a good runner.

Eleri felt cut up over the split, but she was glad she was free to make her own decisions on love and life. Some of her friends who were in religions had been fucked over in her mind, mainly by blokes making decisions on their behalf in a weird patriarchy. She thought most religions made their followers into fantasists, often making them look upon people outside of their religion in a derogatory or bigoted manner, and most of them seemed to discriminate against women one way or another.

Eleri thought that Osian liked her, but he was a bit too shy to say so and if anything happened between them, she was concerned that if it went badly it would affect their friendship. So, it had been left as one of the long-term simmering 'could have beens'. She had feelings for him as strong as she had had for anyone, but the stars had never quite aligned for them, with one of them usually seeing someone else when the other person was available.

They'd also had a few years where they had struggled to stay in touch much when Osian was seeing Sian, who was something of a green-eyed monster. She hadn't liked Osian having much, if any, contact with women other than their mums. Osian had become, necessarily, quite a different person during that period, and Eleri had seen Sian pretty much punch Osian out of a pub when he'd been chatting to Isabelle for less than a minute. Most people had found it funny at the time, but obviously not poor Osian. When they finally split up, he metamorphosised in the same way that King Theoden in Lord of the Rings did when Gandalf rid him of Wormtongue's spell.

After her split from Jacob, Eleri got even more into her work, a kind of love in itself, looking at how debt affected individuals, and how people could end up locked in 'problem debt'. She wasn't around North Wales very much for a while, and both her and Osian knuckled down, focusing on their work like hermits.

Behind the statistics of debt were individuals such as your close family members and friends, crippled by anxiety about how they are going to pay. It made Eleri white with rage when she heard some politicians dismissed these issues and 'othered' the people who were struggling and reducing peoples' dignity.

It often created a stigma around benefits that deterred people from collecting things like disability assistance that would make such a difference to their lives. People with a disability were held back from decent living standards by many different constraints, and over a million unpaid carers also lived in poverty despite the vital role they play in society.

Debt deductions, particularly the repayable advance many people were often forced to take out to sort the long weeks of waiting for Universal Credit, seemed to be a prime example of how people ended up destitute.

*

She'd met some great people on her travels and made some new friends. After her break up with Jacob, she hungout with her friend Hannah in Manchester a good deal, often in a dark back bar in one of the pubs on Burton Road. Hannah had been a good shoulder to lean on, a few years older than Eleri with long dark hair, olive skin and an oft broad smile on her face, she seemed to like hearing about Eleri's relationship woes and it felt to Eleri like having a form of counsel. Hannah was a born and bred Mancunian, and drank more booze than anyone else Eleri had spent time with. She would often text Eleri the morning afterwards, "I'm so hungover today, I'm never drinking again," but it was a standard message to receive twice a week.

Outside of the booze and crack, Hannah was brilliant at her job, creating clothing ranges and exhibitions for an organisation which was a representative body for climbers and walkers. She often sorted Eleri out with free T-shirts, and had given her some good ideas for what to look into around some of her work and research matters.

Hannah said she was going to leave her job soon. It had been a good place to work once, apparently, but was changing a lot, and not for the better, with the appearance of a few very highly paid managers who were clueless and didn't give a shit about staff. Eleri thought Hannah was making a safe move in leaving.

Every time Eleri left Manchester, her liver sighed with relief as Hannah's excess drinking definitely rubbed off on Eleri when they hungout together.

*

Penny Hunter was another new friend and lived in the Centre of Birmingham. Penny had striking ginger hair, a strong brummy accent, a sharp wit and had been wheelchair-bound for much of her life. Eleri had been looking into different rates of disability benefits in regions and Penny had offered insights into what this meant in reality and had been up for an interview.

CHAPTER 6:
Y WRAIGYN Y GADAIROLWYN (THE WOMAN IN THE WHEELCHAIR)

Penny worked in a library, was a voracious reader of sci-fi and fantasy books, and had an infectious laugh. She also had a firm grip, with tough hands that had grown very strong over years of pushing herself around. They'd gone for a drink after the first interview, and if Eleri was ever in Birmingham after that first meeting, she would always stay with Penny. Eleri had introduced her to techno, and she had taken to it with a keen ear, even coming out to a few nights in North Wales.

Concerning people with different disabilities, Penny knew people could be clueless in terms of understanding how different the world could be for her and for them. She needed excellent public transport links for events and work, and a lot of buildings weren't set up with a ramp for her to enter, or a lift to get her onto different floors.

People would often look at her with pity, which really did her head in as Penny loved life more than most people who didn't require a wheelchair to get around. Penny had been brought up by her mum, Juliet, as her dad had left before she was born, and she had never known him. Her mum had been a lovely woman who taught Penny to look after herself and to have high aspirations even though they had very little.

When her mum had died, she was 16. She was morose for some time and felt lonely as fuck. It was November, the start of winter, and very wet and windy. Since then, November had been the worst time of the year for Penny. Her mum had taken her everywhere and they'd just hangout most evenings, watching TV and chatting rubbish. They'd watch the horrors and sci-fis that were on Channel 4 that usually started at 10pm and would go on for hours.

After a few months of being super down, Penny remembered what her mum had taught her; to set her mind to a task and focus on that thing until it was finished, not to worry about failure, but to try as hard as she possibly could again and again. It was with this attitude that she gained some A-levels and, after becoming a part-time librarian, managed to live independently. This was after a few visits to the Citizens Advice bureau, who were great, and put her in the direction of Disability Rights UK who helped her out.

*

Penny had never left Birmingham before she met Eleri, but since then she'd done a couple of journeys over to North Wales to visit Eleri and had made a load of new friends. It was such a different world from the concrete of Birmingham. She'd not realised the delights to be found in music like techno too. When she got back from Wales after the nights out, she always went through different Decomposed Radio episodes in the evenings after work, reminiscing back to the nights and wondering when she could next make it over.

She was sad her mum wasn't alive to go over there too. Smoking had caught up with her mum sooner rather than later, with lung cancer being the killer. She'd tried to get her mum to stop, and she didn't like Eleri and her friends smoking. It's one of the easier ways to leave the world early, other than driving like a twat or committing suicide.

*

The first trip Penny had done to Wales was when Eleri had taken her over for a weekend trip. They'd gone in her slightly screwed Ford Escort, which Eleri spent a lot of time slagging off on the way over. As they got onto the A5, the journey was amazing through Llangollen, windows open and sun streaming in. Eleri played one of the Decomposed Radios; 047. Penny was hooked after the first 15 minutes, and the music seemed to put a smile on Eleri's face. They'd stayed at Eleri's parents' house in Deiniolen. It was at that point she realised Eleri and her parents really were Welsh.

Ray: "Iawn Eleri? Pwy'di hi?"

Eleri: "Gweddol, diolch dad. Dyma Penny, ffrind fi o Birmingham."

Gwawr: "Croeso i Gyrmu Penny! That means welcome to Wales."

Penny: "You really are Welsh Eleri! I've never heard Welsh before, it sounds lovely."

Gwawr: "It's our first language here. It's a very old language you know."

Gwawr made them all tea and asked about her life in Birmingham, which she gave an overview of.

Gwawr: "We call a library 'llyfrgell' in Welsh. It must be nice having so many books around!"

Penny: "It is. It's also pretty good exercise to be honest, as I spend a lot of time shuttling about, putting books back and organising. I only get to read when it's very quiet."

The front door opened, Gwawr's eyes lit up and Eleri got up and hugged the young man who walked through, wearing very dirty looking clothes. Eleri had chatted a bit to Penny about

Jordan, and he was as she'd imagined him; sharp eyes, dark hair and a slightly cheeky look about him. He looked strong too.

Eleri: "Penny, this is my little brother Jordan."

Jordan smiled and waved at Penny.

Penny: "Nice to meet you Jordan. Looks like you've been working hard today?"

Jordan: "Looks like I've been mud fighting more like! Great to meet you too, I hear you've got a taste for techno."

Gwawr: "Oh no, she's not been busting your ear drums with that stuff, has she?"

Penny: "Ha! I liked it, thanks Gwawr. It's like the opposite of classical!"

Jordan: "Fancy hearing some more of it Penny? There's a night on at Hendre Hall tomorrow, Eleri?"

Penny: "I'd be keen."

Eleri: "Sounds great to me, not been out in ages. Gonna be back late mum, sorry! Is it still ok to use our old room? Penny can have Megan's old bunk."

Gwawr: "Of course, that's what I'd expected."

Penny felt glad to be taken into the household like a family member and to sleep in the girls' old room.

*

The next day, Penny, Eleri and Jordan went out through the slate quarry, from Bus Stop to a lookout over Llanberis and the mountains. Eleri explained along the way how her and her friends climbed on some of the facets. Gwawr made them pysgod a sglodion (fish and chips) later on, before they went out for a beer at a pub Penny couldn't remember the name of. She met some of Eleri's friends who were going to Hendre too; Zoe, Isabelle et al.

Eleri drove Penny and Jordan to Hendre, where there were a couple of DJs who were well-known in the techno community, Lisa and Ben. Penny saw Jordan have a dip in a bag and soon later he disappeared and seemed to be having a great time. Penny had her chair quite near the front and Eleri danced near her for much of the night. Penny was taken by the energy of the night. Eleri drove them back when it finished at 2am, but Jordan stayed out, going to some friend's house.

Eleri: "Nice to have a night that finishes pretty early for a change!"

Penny was glad of a bed at that point. She said her goodbyes to Gwawr and Ray the day after, and Eleri and her set off back down the A5 towards Birmingham and work. Jordan still hadn't resurfaced from the night before.

Penny: "What was it that Jordan took last night at Hendre?"

Eleri: "MDMA, ecstacy. It's very nice and makes you want to dance. Gives you a lot of energy."

Penny: "I'd like to try some if there's a chance sometime."

Eleri: "Sure, next time we're up and there's a night on, we'll do some and get a taxi back to wherever we stay. Just be warned, it keeps you awake, and you don't want to take too much or else you'll have a come down a few days later. It uses a lot of your serotonin on the night. A point to remember when taking it is to start low and go slow; you don't need much."

Penny: "I sleep badly most of the time anyway, but good shout about the amount. I don't intend to go too crazy."

Penny felt jubilant about the weekend; it had been such a great time. Work back in the library in Birmingham felt like a bit of a comedown, and she messaged Eleri about when they could do it again. It sounded like Eleri was on the rebound after a relationship and needed some friends to lean on.

Soon after she had entered Eleri's circle of friends, Osian

had taken it upon himself to build Penny a more versatile wheelchair - what he called a 'roamer chair'. He had only made two others over the years, so Eleri had seen the prototypes. The majority of wheelchairs were only good for flat, hard areas, such as pavements and roads, but were often crap on grass fields, getting stuck easily and being tough to push. The roamer chair had bigger and thicker mountain-bike-like wheels which made it great for going a bit more off-road. Penny had made some circuits up near where she lived, going across parks and on some pretty rights of way she could access via bus routes that she'd never have been able to before. On another trip to Wales, Eleri and Jordan had helped her get around Llyn Idwal, which had some fantastic mountain landscapes all around it. She saw climbers going up the Idwal slabs, which she thought looked like a big triangle of cheese.

*

Each time Penny got back to Birmingham, life seemed a little bit greyer and, over the years, she started to feel more and more strain with everyday life.

Penny had always lived pretty frugally. Her small ground floor flat was cheap as far as rent went. She did the same £30 food shop at Lidl every week which normally did her fine, but then a time came when, between a combination of reduced benefit and increased prices, the £30 didn't cover the food. With no savings, Penny had limited options, so cut out the cheese and pickle sandwiches she normally liked to have for lunch. After a few months of this, she realised she was going to get into debt without some drastic measures and for her this meant going to a foodbank. She had put it off as long as she could and hated the idea of using one. It felt like charity to her, and she'd prided herself on her independence all her life.

It was a Monday night, a week before she was due to be paid, that she wheeled herself down to the foodbank and joined the short queue of people waiting. It was a small ground floor building between a Smith's and a Barnardo's. Penny felt people's pitying stares on her and some of the others in the queue as they went past, and she nearly wheeled herself off with the deep feeling of shame she felt. Just ahead of her, a greying lady in a brown woolly jumper and jeans stood with two young children, a boy and a girl. The boy was blonde and the girl was slightly ginger, like Penny. She gave them all a smile. The woman smiled back and said:

"First time here? We've only been coming the last few weeks."

Penny: "It is. I've been putting it off, but I don't get paid for a week and I've not got much food left in. Everything seems so expensive!"

"Sorry you are out of food, all part of their 'big society' eh? I'm Barbara, and this is Celyn and Robert."

Penny: "I'm Penny, nice to meet you all."

Robert asked: "How long have you been in a wheelchair?"

Penny: "As long as I can remember!"

Robert: "I'm sorry about that."

Penny laughed: "I'm used to it, but thanks Robert."

Eventually Penny came to be inside where a lovely, industrious woman called Dee welcomed her and handed her a bag full of random tins of fruit and veg, some pasta, rice, tea and soup. Penny thanked her as she placed each item into the canvas bag hanging off the side of her wheelchair. She said goodbye to Barbara, Celyn and Robert, and made her way out and back home, avoiding the pitying eyes of some of the people walking past as she left.

As she wheeled herself down the street towards the bus station, she knew that from then on she would be needing to do this same journey to the foodbank every month and get used to the pitying eyes. Thinking back to the nice food she used to eat, like her cheese and pickle sandwiches for lunch, it was looking likely to be a thing of the past. Bollocks, she thought, as her tummy grumbled hungrily and the wind picked up and started to make her fingers feel numb.

When she got home, she cooked the pasta and threw in some tinned carrots, sweetcorn and a cuppa soup for some flavouring. She was hungry as hell, so it tasted pretty good. Hunger can make a lot of things taste good.

She watched the TV that night and there were a few things on. Her mind stuck on two slightly negative items, as human minds tend to be drawn. One was the advertisements for nice food, which she was now unlikely to ever be able to afford again, unless some miracle happened.

The second was a government minister. A round, red-faced Conservative MP was trying to explain that benefit 'scroungers' were the causes of many of the country's ills. Penny thought balefully about him, and eventually managed to get him and his shitty unevidenced ideas out of her mind, taking pity on him, as he did come across as profoundly thick.

Her trips to the foodbank went from monthly to weekly, which helped to balance her accounts so she wouldn't be spiralling too far into debt too soon. She enjoyed chatting to Barbara, Celyn and Robert, but she always felt uncomfortable about her trip to the foodbank, like some of her dignity had been taken away from her.

CHAPTER 7: FFRIND (A FRIEND)

Zoe Bud knew how to enjoy life for sure. Why not go through life with a smile on your face when it was so short anyway? When Zoe walked into a room, she brought a positive energy that rubbed off on people. She'd gone into journalism for the Daily Post for a laugh at first, when she'd finished her English lit degree at Bangor University. The Daily Post seemed so fantastically xenophobic, she thought it would be funny to meet the bigoted people who worked there and try to mellow them out a bit. Always harping on about tourists and 'people from somewhere else', they sounded a bit like a local version of UKIP.

During her first week, she realised the people who worked there were actually ok, just like the people you'd find in the pub, but the fact was, divisive shit sells. They loved slagging off people going for a walk up Snowdon, or people parking their vans in laybys. Zoe had tried to explain to them that tourism is good for the economy, and that their family and relatives might be relying on these people coming to the area. Cafes, BnBs, taxis, cleaners, wardens, attractions, guiding... there was an exhaustive list of jobs which these people helped support by coming to the area.

She once got chatting to Dafydd, who had been one of the main writers at the paper for the last 15 years and therefore held a level of responsibility for the crap tone. He was a fairly large, rotund man with a bald head and greying wisps of hair here and there that brushed his big red nose. He was somewhere in his fifties, and made Zoe think more of a farmer than a journo.

Zoe: "How would you like it if your mum went to Scotland, walked up Ben Nevis, and got talked about in a derogatory way in a newspaper up there, like you do about tourists here?"

Dafydd mumbled something Zoe couldn't make out, before saying: "Mum doesn't go away on holiday."

Zoe: "Well I'm sure some of your relatives do! The tourists here are somebody's relatives and you talk about them like they're shit, because they're an easy target."

Dafydd: "They cause all sorts of problems! Poo, bad parking, pissing off the farmers."

Zoe: "These are manageable problems found in any nice tourist area all over the world. Some places have toilets, bins, educational signs, farmers who open their fields for parking and camping, etc."

Dafydd: "They don't speak our language, or know our ways of doing things."

Zoe: "So you think that because someone knows a certain language or lives in a different postcode, it makes them a worse human being than someone who speaks that particular language or was born on a particular piece of land. Is that what you are saying?"

Dafydd: "That may be what I'm saying and although it's not good, it is what I think and it's what a lot of our readers think, or at least want to read about."

Zoe: "You do realise that people are pretty much the same wherever you find them? They look similar, act similar, they have the same desires and faults. Your attitude is the reason people fight wars in the end. It seems fantastically small-minded to me. I think the whole concept of countries should be abolished, and in terms of language and the names for things, does it really matter what anything is called in the end? Surely in a thousand years, none of the languages we know today will be the same and, with our smart phones, pretty soon we could have a chat with anyone from anywhere in the world and it will translate it for us."

Dafydd: "Good luck with that dear. If we got rid of nations, how would we decide the teams for rugby? Words and language have a power too. The Welsh language will be here forever."

Zoe stuck her tongue out at Dafydd, who smiled back.

Dafydd: "They've nearly always got fancy cars too, compared to the people who live around here."

Zoe: "Have you actually done any research to check that, or is it your assumption?"

Dafydd: "You could do the research to back it up now you're here, keep our paper 'evidence-based'. Whilst you are at it, you could look at the problem of second homes in the area. They are destroying our communities. People want to live next to neighbours, not empty buildings, and it has meant young local people can't afford to buy a house, often getting gazumped by people from the city."

Zoe: "Which city? But yeah, I know what you mean about second homes, it does seem a big issue, particularly down the Llŷn Peninsula at Abersoch, eh? House prices are nuts there. I have a friend from the Lake District though, and he said they have the same problem up there so it's not just here."

Dafydd: "Good point about Abersoch. There are some other towns as bad, I think. We could do a story with a load of interviews with locals from these bad areas..."

Zoe sighed quietly as Dafydd droned on, finding his rhythm in his usual way of slagging off people from outside his area.

Zoe tried to change the constant moaning narrative by putting out some more positive news stories, about new jobs created, young people who had set up successful new businesses, farmers that had expanded out of their normal agricultural activities and had embraced the tourism industry somehow. Most people enjoyed chatting to Zoe and opened up with stories. Her old man had taught her how to use a camera pretty well too, which helped with pictures to accompany the stories. Zoe was pretty happy with her life; she had a fun and creative job and a lot of friends in the area. Her little sister Ruby had recently 'come of age' and had joined her on some nights out. She even seemed to handle all-nighters better than some of the more seasoned gremlins.

She missed living with Eleri. It had been a very fun few years, apart from her and Jacob being a bit soppy. Zoe was glad they'd broken up in all honesty, even if Eleri had taken it badly for a time. Zoe thought Jacob was a bit of a lush and had something of a wandering eye when he was drunk. Not that she'd expressed these views to Eleri.

Zoe had recently got a two-bedroom house in Cwm Y Glo, only a fifteen-minute walk from where she and Eleri had once lived in Brynrefail. It was a sweet little village and the pizzas and social at the Fricsan were excellent. Zoe was glad Eleri was going to finally settle back in the area, being Zoe's bestie. Life seemed a little duller when she wasn't around, and she was also killer with the curries she cooked up.

They had a catch-up at Eleri's new house in Llanberis when she was back from her city work. An evening, just the two of them, cosy in the living room near the fire, with a bottle or two of wine.

"What are you working on at the minute Zoe? Any cool stories?" Eleri asked, throwing more wood onto the fire.

Zoe: "A lot of local education authorities are getting nailed due to the crash and related austerity. I'm working on a piece about how this is reducing opportunities for young people to access the outdoors, something which is already harder than when we were kids."

Eleri: "Good effort, it is bad isn't it? The bankers cause the crash, and the kids are paying for it."

Zoe: "Way of the world I guess, but yeah, seems wrong to me. I hope not too many more outdoor centres end up closing or laying off staff, I'm not sure what can take their place. The buildings are usually in such lovely locations too."

Eleri: "They'll probably end up getting flogged and made into hotels that charge a ton."

Zoe: "I'll make sure to make that a cover of the Daily Post if it happens. Dafydd would love that kind of story, especially if it was owned by people in London! I was thinking about resurrecting an old story too, related to that time in the quarries when you nearly blew us all up. You know the plaque opposite the Fricsan, commemorating the explosion in 1869 which killed six people? Two guys were carrying two tons of nitro-glycerine, but it was a hot day and, on the outskirts of Cwm Y Glo, it blew up, killed the two carters, a quarryman, and two young lads too. It left two craters 10 feet deep. A wheel and a cart landed half a mile away and they say the blast might have been the loudest man-made explosion ever heard up until that point. Pretty nuts, eh?"

Eleri's cheeks glowed red from the wine and the fire, brown eyes shining through her round spectacles. She looked vibrant to Zoe.

Eleri: "That is nuts, a tragedy of times past. Who'd have thought it, with it seeming such a sleepy village nowadays? I'd heard something about that before but didn't realise six people had died."

Zoe: "Yeah, it blew a lot of the roofs off the houses too, and most windows. How about you, any good work news?"

Eleri: "In Wales, I guess so. I'll be going down to Cardiff to chat with some people in the Senedd. Wales is, at the end of the day, pretty socialist and will try to look out for people. England is looking screwed though, totally pissing on the poor. You know Penny in Birmingham? She's on the sharp end with getting crapped on. On average, people with a disability face extra costs of around £500 per month related to their condition, and it's not been remotely easy for people like Penny in the current climate."

Zoe: "That's shit, I really like Penny. Hope she's doing ok, and let me know if there is anything we can do to help. On a more optimistic note, how about romance now that you've settled for a bit? Bet they are queueing up! Have you caught up with Osian at all?"

Eleri: "No joy, not that I've been looking. Too busy with work the last few months, or rather years, and getting this house sorted. I've been slack on seeing family too, not caught up with Jordan, Megan or mum and dad for a bit. I'm hoping to change that once I'm fully settled back into the area. I've been getting the odd message that's a bit too friendly off the odd guy who has a partner. I'm definitely not getting involved in that scene though, Jesus. I'll be keen to catch up with Osian too, it sounds like he has become something of a hermit living in his workshop recently. What about you, any news?"

"Same," she lied, blushing slightly. She'd had a brief fling but didn't want to tell Eleri about it, nor anyone else for that matter, but she didn't think Eleri would be too psyched. There may have been a few other people who wouldn't be too psyched too. Zoe had been out with Lewis for a few years, but it was when he was very into his weed and this started to do her head in eventually. He'd prefer to get baked more than have a shag and was so forgetful – the little dickhead forgot it was her birthday one time! He looked to be doing well for himself nowadays though, and Zoe was chuffed for him. Hiking about the Carneddau mountains, looking after the place, sounded a grand way to make a living. He'd started to distance himself from Zoe since he was seeing Bryony, which Zoe thought was fair play.

Zoe: "I like being single at the minute, having the freedom to do what I want, having my own place in Cwm without someone making a mess I have to clean up, or being a jealous pratt."

Eleri: "Or getting baked all the time like Lewis. You make some good points to be fair. I felt really lonely for a while when I split with Jacob and worried about him a lot, but feel a bit like you now. Quite a few friends of ours look like they'd be better off on their own too. I remember going through a period of self-reflection after splitting up and being a bit ashamed about how I behaved, or decisions I'd made when with Jacob. You ever had it when you look back and wonder why you were like that? Places he'd want to go and I just said 'no'. He had started to annoy me mind, which may have been a factor. You need to be able to look warmly at a partner's faults for a relationship to work, and I'd definitely started to fail at that."

Zoe: "I wouldn't worry about that stuff, it's water under the bridge now. I know your family would love to catch up with you. Jordan's been struggling a bit recently I think, not seen him down the pub that much."

Eleri: "Struggling? I have been away too much. I'll give him a call tomorrow."

Zoe: "Small bit of gossip. I heard Georgina is getting divorced. Her partner slept with their aupair. Remember that time when she was being horrendous in Mafon and we put a laxative in her and her friend's brew?"

Eleri went quiet for a few seconds.

Eleri: "*You* put the laxatives in… but you did have my blessing at the time. I feel really sorry for her about the split. Separating from a long-term partner is a shitty thing for anyone. You know, she apologised for how she was when she was younger, at that first party Jordan put on." Eleri thought back and talked through it to Zoe.

*

Eleri had left the buildings full of music and people to get some fresh air, a bit of quiet and a ciggy. She went around the side of one of the buildings to find a young woman sat with her back against the wall, smoking and crying. She didn't look in a great state. It was Georgina Booth. Eleri was very surprised to see her, the first time in many years. Who the fuck had told her about the party?

"Are you ok? It's me, Eleri," she said, bending down.

"Eleri, I'm sorry about how I was when I was younger," Georgina sighed, looking up at her.

Eleri wondered if she'd taken any acid, then sat next to Georgina and shared some of her rollie.

Eleri: "Everyone does stuff they regret, particularly when they are young and finding their feet. Thanks for saying sorry though. I hope you're not crying about that?"

Slowly, Georgina explained that after moving to London she'd started to see a guy who was very controlling. They were living together, but over the last few months he'd started to scare her, and she felt alone as fuck. She hadn't made many new friends where she was living, and it was tricky to do as her partner was very jealous.

Eleri was a bit too high to offer great advice, but after listening to Georgina, she informed her that she should probably think about getting rid of the dickhead, then gave her a third of a pill. Later that night they were dancing together, having a great night.

It had made Eleri's night to make a very surprising peace with someone she'd struggled with over the years, and it made her see Georgina in a totally different light. Admittedly, the drugs may have been helping the both of them. She remembered thinking she hoped Georgina had gotten rid of her partner as it sounded a profoundly negative scene. It can be hard to see how crap it is when in a relationship sometimes, and splitting up could be very tough too.

Zoe listened to Eleri's story then spurt out:

"Jesus, how did I not clock that? I was there, wasn't I?"

Eleri: "I think you were having too good a night to notice much! It was busy that night too. I sincerely hope it's not the same dickhead she was with then that she had kids with and has fucked her over now."

Zoe: "Yeah, you'd have thought not. At least if it is, she'll be free of him soon."

Zoe and Eleri continued chewing the cud into the early hours before they crashed out together, temporary bed friends like when they were younger. Zoe felt a bit dialled from the red wine and spent some time listening to Eleri's quiet snoring as she drifted into sleep.

CHAPTER 8: FY MRAWD (MY BROTHER)

"Thanks for being such a great group. Hope the journey back to Bedford goes well!" Jordan shouted, as the kids he'd been working with for the week piled onto the coach.

It was always a relief when the week ended and all the young people disappeared to be looked after by someone else. During the past week at the outdoor centre, they had taken kids up Yr Wyddfa, climbed on small outcrops near the centre called Lion Rock, gone coasteering on Anglesey and ascended a ghyll scramble up Afon Ddu. A real adventurous week for young people giving some of them an eye into a wild world they'd never experienced before, unless they had parents who had a keen personal interest.

There had been some funny kids on this particular week. Jethro and Tom being total drama queens on the walk up to the top of Snowdon, slowing everyone down by at least an hour. The pair of them often sitting down together and asking: "Is it much further?", "I might have a heart attack if I go any further!" and "This is child abuse Jordan!"

Jordan: "Not too much longer, it's just round the next corner." It wasn't a total lie, but you did have some big aspect changes in the mountains.

Jethro and Tom did make it to the top and came into their own on the ghyll scramble, always wanting to be first on the jumps and chutes into pools.

Blue Peris, based in Dinorwig, was a local education authority for Bedfordshire. Jordan had done a two-year trainee scheme with them, learning the ropes so to speak, gaining his Mountain Leader and Single Pitch Climbing Award then they'd asked him to stay on afterwards. He'd actually lived in the centre itself and it was a beautiful spot crouched between Dinorwig Slate Quarry and Fachwen, which was a hillside full of sessile oak woodland, overlooking Llyn Padarn. He'd felt very grateful for being able to live in such a place.

Eleri had given him some direction towards this move, when Jordan had been feeling a bit lost and pretty down about the labouring work he was doing. He felt he owed her for helping him get this job that he quite liked. She'd gone out of her way to take him out and teach him key safety skills for climbing, often on easy climbs he knew she'd find a bit boring compared with the stuff she did with Lewis and Osian. He was closer with Eleri than with anyone else pretty much. She seemed to get him and his moods, and he was proud of what she'd achieved academically and with her work. He felt rather lacking in ambition by comparison.

He got on well with Carlo who managed the centre, and Carlo always seemed appreciative of Jordan's work. Jordan generally got on well with people, especially the kids who came to the centre.

Carlo: "Nice one this week Jordan. They looked a handful, some of them."

Jordan: "Thanks Carlo. Always easier later in the week once they've gotten warmed into things."

Carlo: "Any plans for the weekend?"

Jordan: "Probably hangout with Becky, but no plans."

Carlo: "Say hi to Becky and have a great weekend. Catch you Monday!"

Jordan: "Cheers Carlo, have a good one too."

As he left the centre, Jordan made a rollie and lit it. When he was younger he was very against smoking. Someone had come into his school and had explained how terrible they were for you. After that he'd started to bin packets of cigarettes when one of his friends had them. He figured he was doing them a favour, even though they didn't see it that way.

His mind changed sometime in his early twenties though, when a lot of his friends were smoking. He'd received a dental bill and was struggling to pay it. Feeling stressed, he went up to a get-together in Dinorwig at Mushroom Bob's house, who he didn't know very well. A few of his friends were there - Sue, Will, John - standing outside the house and all enjoying a drink and smoking. Jordan turned to the tall and gangly Will, and asked:

"Can I have one of them please?"

Will: "You don't smoke! It's not a good idea you know…"

Jordan smiled: "Come on, I've had a stressy week Will."

Will rolled one for him and Jordan puffed his way through it. At first it was only a few at pubs on weekends, but before long Jordan was a smoker, having one with his morning tea, one before bed and shitloads in between. The thing about being a smoker is that there is rarely a bad time to smoke, even though you know it leads to a 'slow and painful death'. Jordan had even had one friend die of emphysema, and another of lung cancer. He knew it was one of the least logical things you could do, but it didn't stop him and many of his friends from doing it. Daft as fuck, the lot of them.

*

Jordan had been seeing Becky for a good few years. She had short blonde hair and a northern accent and worked as a cleaner in the Victoria Hotel in Llanberis. They'd met there when Jordan had been having a pint in the bar with some friends. She'd just finished work and got chatting with them all, but took a particular shine to Jordan. They dated for a while and soon moved in together into a house on Goodman street. They were still there now.

Jordan headed down to the village, parked his white Golf and hustled into the living room. Becky was sat on the rug by the fire.

Becky: "How was your day?"

Jordan: "Not bad thanks. There was almost too much water in the Afon Ddu to get up it but just got away with it. What about you?"

Becky: "Same old, got all the rooms ready for the next load of people arriving tonight."

Jordan sat down next to Becky and made a rollie.

Jordan: "What do you fancy doing tomorrow?"

Becky: "Not sure during the day, but we could go to the cinema in the evening?"

Jordan: "What's on?

Becky: "Frozen, Gravity and Anchorman 2, not sure what else."

Jordan: "Sounds better than banging my head in the door all night."

Becky: "Yeah, yeah, you'll like it. You can choose."

Jordan: "As long as it's not Frozen, I don't mind!"

*

They weren't perhaps the best suited couple. Becky wanted kids, Jordan didn't think he did, or that they could afford them. Jordan liked the odd rave, Becky didn't, Becky seemed 'all in' whereas Jordan just didn't feel that way. But, like with many relationships, proximity and alcohol had led to them hooking up. Jordan had some dark moods sometimes, lasting for months even, and appreciated he was lucky that Becky could put up with them.

He chatted with Eleri about this stuff and had sometimes ended up back at her house after a techno night when she wasn't away working. Everyone would go to sleep eventually, apart from Eleri and Jordan, and then he'd hike back home to see Becky, if she wasn't at work.

When he was a trainee at Blue Peris, Jordan had organised a rave himself. Plenty of his friends were DJs and Blue Peris had a generator out back for various bits of building work on its grounds. After climbing with Eleri one day in the quarry, she had shown him the Pumphouse. There were three decently sized rooms, with some funky old machinery in two of them. The middle room, however, had a floor which looked like a it could be a goer for dancing on. He was sure he'd heard his dad mention he'd been to a rave here many years ago. There was a lot of goat shit, but it was old and didn't stink too much, at least not to him. It had taken Jordan two days of work to clean it up enough for a party though.

A few nights before, he'd gone there at night and it was just him and thirty-odd goats, most staring at him. It seemed as though they were wondering why he was in their realm, their oval eyes cooly regarding Jordan and creeping him out a little. They eventually took the hint and headed out, leaving Jordan to his hard work of shovelling their shit out of the way.

His friends Jon and Steve had come for a bit, to help do the final clean on the day. Jordan taxed three rollies off them in the space of an hour, and Jon and Steve had a spliff each for every rollie Jordan had. He didn't know how they managed it with the joints looking to be ten times the size of his rollies.

Cleaning out the building had reminded Jordan of his days labouring for Paddy. Paddy always managed to find the hardest jobs, facing houses with large rocks in the middle of winter, digging drainage trenches when the weather was truly grim. They were working on a job for half a year on the coast once, on a complex of three-story sandstone buildings. A truck would deliver a load of mud and rocks, Jordan would pull the better rocks out, 'coin' them with a hammer and chisel, heave them up to the right level on the scaffold, and mix cement and bucket that up too. Paddy would cement the rocks up against the breeze blocks and make sure it looked good. If it was too cold, the cement wouldn't set properly. Indoor jobs during the winter would have been much more preferable. Sometimes Jordan would have to rearrange the scaffolding for parts of the job and Paddy told him not to fall off it as the insurance would be void. There must be a ton of accidents in construction work like this, Jordan thought. He also remembered being blown away by Paddy's memory for Radio Two's 'Popmaster', rarely getting a question wrong.

Jordan had never been stronger than during those brutal six months, and he was reminded of this as he struggled to carry the generator down to the Pumphouse the night before the rave. He carried it like a rucksack, and accidentally carried it the wrong way up, sloshing petrol and oil around. He realised much later that it wasn't such a great idea. He'd arranged with other friends that they would carry other key pieces of equipment on the night and he burned some incense to try and get rid of the smell of goat shit.

You needed two people to carry each speaker, two for a sub, you also needed a mixer and every DJ wanted to bring their own controller. You also needed good lasers. Then a smoke machine, the fluid for it and perhaps even a hazer. Everything you took in, you needed to get back out again when people were going to be very tired. A lot of people definitely didn't clock what went into a rave. This was a small one, but still involved almost twenty people to set up and derig overall.

He'd arranged with the set-up crew to meet at the Pumphouse

at 8.30pm, but for over an hour it was just Jordan and an owl hooting somewhere in the eaves of the building. Eventually some of the crew turned up and something of a 'Time Team' style build of the music-, laser- and smoke-system ensued.

When Jon arrived without a long extension lead, Jordan thought the job was screwed as the generator was 30 metres away from the music equipment, but luckily Nathan heard and brought one up. Jordan had arranged with seven of his friends to DJ.

There was a small table made of iron in one corner of the dance room which made a perfect DJ table. After a lot of running around stressing, Jordan sighed with relief when he walked through one of the doorways, after having a rollie outside, to find the music pumping. It had taken five people 45 minutes just to get the generator working. After he'd carried it the wrong way up, it was a bit screwed, but it was finally up and running. Eleri came up to Jacob and gave him a hug, before offering prosecco. She'd brought up a load of fairy lights to add to the atmosphere.

Eleri: "Well done!"

Jordan: "Thanks Eleri, let's hope the night comes off with no epics."

Eleri: "Christ, I never thought I'd come to a party up here after how gross it seemed a few years ago."

They'd helped Penny get to the Pumphouse, some local youths lending a hand with manoeuvring her wheelchair. She was sound, Jordan thought, and he was chuffed that she'd decided to come.

Zoe and Isabelle arrived and gave Jordan a hug before they shared out a bag of MDMA to dab on. By midnight the dance floor was packed and, at numerous points, everyone was trying their best to hit the roof. Steve's set was impressive. He lived for music and had the crowd in his hands.

Occasionally, Jordan would go out for a smoke and a chat in the hangout room, where the huge old machinery sat. On one such respite, Jordan looked up and saw Smiler looking in, his face its usual fascinatingly painful grimace, the face of someone who lived in the deepest possible pain.

Jordan: "You're welcome to come and join us."

But no sooner had the words come out of his mouth, than Smiler turned away and headed off somewhere into the night. Jordan found the contrast between Smiler's misery and the happiness the masses were having in the night tricky to deal with but figured another dab or two would sort him out.

Most of the night was spent dancing. Maisy and Jenny, brilliant local artists and circus performers, were always at the front, an unstoppable pair of friends. Osian with his shaggy blonde hair bouncing had an arm over his friend Morus' back, a guy with the biggest sideburns and mullet Jordan had ever seen. Osian shouted "this is Wales!" to him. It was indeed Wales. Will Dixon was having a great night, as ever. Jordan had first met him at a bunker party in the catacombs. Will had come up to him and offered him a pill, and although Jordan didn't know him, he necked it anyway and an hour later had some of the best few hours of his life. They had been friends since then. Timm and Sera, husband and wife, seemed to be loving it too, always psyched for a dance session, Tim was getting into his DJing now too. Zoe's dad, Gareth, was there too and she was sorting him out with some bombs. If Jordan had kids he'd hope his would do the same for him.

When outside again he was surprised to see Eleri talking with Georgina Booth. He'd heard his sister talk about her in not very charitable ways when they were younger, but Jordan put it down to the feel-good effects of the drugs.

Penny had her wheelchair next to the DJ decks most of the night, arms in the air keeping pace with the beats. The arm of her wheelchair came in handy throughout the night to do lines of coke and ket every now and then. Some bottles of Lucozade were doing the rounds too, a very fine dance drink.

It was a shame Becky wasn't into this kind of thing, Jordan thought. He would have liked someone to dance with. Eleri and Jacob were having a proper get down near the front, all over each other. Later in the night, he did notice one woman's eyes a good deal. There was something there for sure; Jordan had the vague memory of something 'almost' happening at one of the bunker parties. The whites of a person's eyes. Jordan had read in a book that animals don't have visible eye whites and that blushing was a uniquely human trait. There was a word Jordan had heard, which was ludicrous to pronounce, that described the moment when two people look at each other with yearning, hoping the other person will initiate something but that neither will.

The dancefloor felt electric to Jordan.

The stories from his childhood such as Arawn and the scenes from the underworld in the Mabinogion couldn't have fitted into the party more. It felt like another world. The smoke, haze, lasers, bodies, beats, drugs, sighs of pleasure, more beats, more drugs. Yeah, Jordan was sure that Arawn, the king of the underworld, would have loved it. If he had existed of course.

Later in the night Jordan brought out a flask of peppermint tea, an extremely useful rave strategy for helping to feel perky and not too rough the next day. Most friends would be grateful for a swig in the later hours.

Theo had been worried about doing the last set of the night, but she shouldn't have been. The dance floor was still packed and the set was blinding. She was Jordan's favourite DJ, with an exceptional ear for rhythm and sometimes a slightly sexual tinge to some of her sets. After about twenty minutes she kicked the bass in and, even listening to the song after the party, Jordan was filled with a warm feeling.

Boom, boom, boom, "Ignition". Deep bass pulsing, dancefloor

erupting as morning emerged.

The synth at 45 minutes was also a fantastic section. A fine ear for music indeed.

When they finally killed the tunes, Jordan looked around at the mess with concern and went outside for a tab and to hang out with the gremlins that were left. A quick shout out for a tidy and five minutes later he went back in to find the place stunningly clean. Jesus, he thought, it's the tidiest the place has been for decades, and idly thought about invoicing the council for the service. It really did deserve being a UNESCO heritage site. It was an eery morning with a mist that Jordan thought was ideal for masking what they all looked like.

Various youths helped carry the equipment down to Llanberis and, after stashing the generator, Jordan joined Eleri and co in helping Penny negotiate the steep steps before they stumbled down to his house in Llanberis. Becky had gone to work and with some mellow music on and a team of party goers who refused to go to sleep, they chatted about the night and shooted the shit. He played them his favourite sets from Decomposed Radio; 003, 005, 037 at 16 minutes in, 047, and the end of 059 really were outstanding pieces of music. Finally, he hit the wall and crashed out.

It was probably the most memorable night he'd had on earth. Amazing music, friends loving it, intense energy on the dance floor and at times a dark undertone which seemed to filter into a lot of the people who ended up in North Wales. It was something Jordan loved about the people, that mercurial element where you weren't sure what they might do, and they rarely put out that hapless constant positivity which many people felt obliged to express in the current age.

*

Jordan had picked up some 'issues' as he'd grown, from moodiness and depression to uncertainty about his relationship, but he doubted he'd find any contentment in another.

He wasn't too sure if he wanted to spend the rest of his life with Becky, in fact he'd even had one affair, just briefly, but an affair nevertheless. He remembered walking back on the quiet side of Llyn Padarn on the way back from that night. What he didn't remember was how it had ended up just being him and her at the end.

They were sat on one of the many rounded, tree-covered rocks that protrude into the lake, sharing a rollie or two and chatting, a very warm feeling buzzing between them and a sense of seclusion as if they were the only people in the world, alone on the side of Llyn Padarn, tiredness helping to reduce inhibition. It felt warm and the lake surface was crystal smooth reflecting the trees nearby.

They'd started kissing at first but soon had to find somewhere in the woods nearby. Finding a clearing, they stumbled into each other, their hands in each other's hair, lips finding skin. When he woke up they were snuggled together, her leg over his stomach, his arm cradling her back between the old oaks and in the mosses and ferns. He lay awake for a while holding her and when she woke there was another strong appetite for sex. They both came at the same time, in sync, which was a rarity for Jordan. After they'd finished, they hung out for a short time, sharing another rollie before going their separate ways.

Jordan wasn't sure what to make of it and he doubted she knew either. They kept it quiet and even on the occasions they saw each other, they didn't speak of it. It was most assuredly not something he was proud of but wasn't something he regretted either. A brief intense connection with someone he got on well with. He knew that dopamine didn't like anything predictable, the more unpredictable the situation was, the bigger the prediction of reward and dopamine release, perhaps adding to the intensity of feelings he'd felt, however morally questionable.

He didn't love Becky and didn't get the feeling she loved him. He wondered idly how many relationships were like his. He had seen people stay together even though they weren't into the other person. They probably just didn't want to be alone, or factors such as children or paying for rent helped keep people together however unhappy they were. He thought it was one of life's small tragedies, the fact that much of human interaction could be so confusing and inefficient.

*

Another key issue for Jordan was his depression. He could probably do with some prescription drugs, but he'd prefer to chop his arm off than do that. He'd spoken with one or two other people who experienced something similar. They spoke of the joylessness of life and it put him on edge hearing them verbalise what he was feeling.

"I'm not looking forward to anything Jordan," His friend said down the phone, crying and forlorn, a lost soul. She sounded screwed but what could he do but empathise; he often felt the same. He wasn't looking forward to anything, his job was one of the few things he liked, perhaps tapping into the enthusiasm of the young.

It was still better than back in school at least. He hadn't liked that much at all. It had felt like being in a jungle. After school one day he had been hanging out with his friend John Loan when they'd been effectively chased into the local garage by a gang of youths. An older boy, Jamie, wanted to have a fight with John for something John had said about his girlfriend. John rightly looked scared in the garage. Jamie had a reputation for being hard and the age difference made it look an unfair fight. After a while of hiding in the garage, an older boy called Dean came in who worked out at the gym a lot. He spoke to John.

Dean: "You don't have to fight him if you don't want."

Fair play to John he said he would face Jamie and came out

of the garage to a quiet field nearby with a small gang of kids watching. The fight didn't go as people expected and John beat the shit out of the older kid. But it was horrible to watch. Getting Jamie on the ground, John, who was well built for his age, sat on top of him and punched his face bloody until he couldn't use his fists. He then started using his elbows until Dean and some of the older kids watching stopped it all. It was an awful scene as far as Jordan was concerned, even if his friend had 'won'. Jamie had been taken to hospital, concussed and needing stitches, perhaps lucky that that was all that was wrong with him.

Yeah, adulthood was better than being a kid for sure, but it could still be totally fucked for so many. Jordan had been vaguely following the news. Something about a banking crisis and the housing bubble bursting.

Gordon Brown: "We need to inject a lot of money into the system to prevent a collapse."

Some names he'd never heard of spoke of "fiscal discipline", "efficiencies to be made", "austerity", and "big society".

It was still some years later and a surprise for Jordan when it finally reached him. Carlo asked him into his office.

Carlo: "I'm really sorry Jordan, Blue Peris aren't going to be able to offer you a contract next year."

Jordan's stomach sank at the news and his face flushed in shame, thinking perhaps he'd done something wrong.

Jordan: "No problem Carlo, what does it mean though? Is there any work for me?"

Carlo: "There will definitely be some work, but it will be on a freelance basis. There won't be quite as much, local education authorities are getting big cuts through everywhere, and many centres are closing. Hopefully it won't come to that here but there are no certainties."

Jordan relaxed a bit hearing that it was down to things that were out of his control.

Jordan: "Ok sound, freelance work will be ok. Nice one."

But it wasn't ok for Jordan. He'd had a salary during the winter with Blue Peris, where he'd do a bit of maintenance work when it was quiet with groups. Without this, work during the winter was quiet, as the weather was often rubbish and that meant it was hard to make any money. Being skint is stressful. Many billions of people around the world will spend much of their lives worrying about being totally skint, concerned with being able to cover the basics.

Jordan did find some temp work in a factory for a company based near Porthmadog but the boss Simon came across as a small-minded bully. Jordan would have preferred to go hungry than work for such a man in the end. He was sure Simon must have some redeeming features as he did have a family, but Jordan had observed none.

Jordan started doing a bit of labouring again, but it felt like taking a step backwards in life and it was only three quarters of the pay of outdoor work, sometimes even less than that.

It put pressure on his and Becky's relationship, something that Jordan thought might well be evaporating without any other external stresses. It started by them not going out as much. They used to go out once a week for a bar meal, in the Glyntwrog or sometimes burgers at the Heights. Rather than this, it was nights in together. They had the odd argument over stuff they bought, where they'd never argued before.

Becky: "We aren't going to be able to afford a family if you go out with your mates and waste all your money on booze!"

Jordan: "I don't want a family anyway, you do."

Becky: "Go fuck yourself."

"It's all I get to do nowadays!" Jordan yelled as he slammed the door on his way out to walk off his frustration, fear and anger.

*

The council tax bills came through the letter box and a sense of dread filled the air. How do you pay for it when your overdraft is maxed out and not much money is coming in for the next month or two? The freelance work Jordan did was always slow to be paid when he put his invoices in, sometimes coming in up to two months later.

It felt like they entered a descending spiral of being more and more skint and being more and more stressed. He knew from his chats with Eleri about debt spirals and the effect living in debt had on mental health and he detested being in the grim position. Jordan started to skip meals to save money and cut down on hot showers, a duo many skint people have adopted for a period of time.

Jordan found that some of his more affluent 'friends' lacked awareness of hard work.

"Long time no hear Jordan!" said Harriet, the daughter of a doctor, not realising Jordan had been struggling to pay for phone top ups for some time and had been drawing money out on a credit card to pay for stuff. He gave her an evil stare as she zoomed off in a fancy car her parents had bought her and thought why the fuck couldn't she have called him, the daft cunt. He had a few friends who came across badly, being extremely wealthy and blind to how lucky they were, believing themselves to have worked hard for it when they were from a background of familial wealth where poverty and the anxiety which was often partnered with it had never touched them.

A cream topping to being skint was leaving the house one day to find his car about to get put onto a breakdown truck. A large bald man was playing with the winch to start to pull it up.

Jordan: "What the hell are you doing? That's my car!"

Big bald guy: "Police said it was on the pavement, asked for it to be towed."

Jordan: "It wasn't on the pavement when I parked it last night, some pissheads must have bunked it onto it"

Big bald guy: "Well it's £100 callout for me pal to get your car back."

Jordan didn't know what to say and scraped together what money he had to retrieve his car. Becky went to the police station later on to explain how skint they were, but the cop didn't listen and came across as a total arse hole. Jordan knew shitty things in life often came in waves, but he was dumbfounded by his run of poor luck with work and money and it was doing his self-esteem and depression no good at all.

Keen for escape in oblivion, Jordan put on another rave in the same place. This one didn't go as smoothly; the amp didn't work and it was a lot busier. There was twice the amount of people as the first he'd done but with no music for the first hour and a half. The set-up team looked stressed. Thinking they were fucked, eventually some random NEDs carried an amp up from Deiniolen. Jordan didn't know who they were but was grateful for their assistance on saving the night.

When the music finally started at around 1am the dancefloor soon became hard to move. It was packed and Jordan remembered little for a few hours apart from spending 10 minutes trying to light a rollie and not managing it. He must have been spangled. Later some of the NEDs who had saved the night with the back-up amp wanted a go on the decks. One guy who had some learning difficulties took over with some kind of psytrance with Theo talking at him by his side, looking concerned at the genre of music.

It all seemed quite nuts to Jordan. Quite a few people seemed to be in a K-hole, temporarily out of action having overcooked the ketamine. Mushroom Bob and some of his crew turned up, one of whom had taken some liquid acid and had to be restrained by some people who knew him outside. Jordan took it off the list of drugs to try and he could see the guy's friends would have their hands full for the evening because the effects of acid could last for twelve or more hours.

The night certainly had a much darker edge to it and when morning came Jordan noticed a guy sat near the back of the dancefloor. He had a warm-looking hat on but his eyes looked like they had a grey goo film over them and around his mouth was almost blue. Jordan thought he was dead.

"Fuck," Jordan thought. He thought about what it would be like to call North Wales Police and say:

"Hi, there is a dead dude at this party I've organised. Can you come and pick him up? He's cramping the dance floor vibes."

This was every party organiser's worst nightmare; a dead dude.

Jordan prodded him with a finger and asked:

"Are you ok?"

The guy moved outside and continued to look critically ill out there. After a bit of time, another guy who seemed to know him and who didn't look as screwed started to try and get him out of the quarries but Jordan wouldn't have put bets on them managing it. It had seemed to Jordan like a scene out of a horror movie. What drugs the guy had taken he could not guess. One of the lost souls of the world, Jordan felt pity for him. In the early hours of a rave when you were very tired people could sometimes appear like gargoyles, but this was really next level stuff.

One of Jordan's friends Jacob, who had helped on the other night, was amused by the scenes of chaos and music. He was always good crack and helped on the clean up when many were too tired and had bailed.

The amp scene led to a blow out between him and Theo. It

had been stressful for both of them, having hundreds of people waiting for music and...there being no music. Jordan had asked her to arrange a backup several times, which would have been easy, but it had clearly gone in one ear and out of the other. She instead blamed Jordan for the lack of back-up amp and garbled on at him in the early hours which he certainly could have done without on the walk out and deconstruction stage.

Christ, it had felt stressful.

*

A few days later him and Becky had food with his parents up in Deiniolen. He was loath to tell them about their financial difficulties and had a fairly profound come down. Why he didn't just pull the 'not feeling too well' card and hidden at home he'd no idea.

Gwawr: "How did the night go you put on?"

Jordan: "How'd you know about that?"

Gwawr: "Everyone knew about this one! They were talking about it in Ray's work, weren't they Ray?"

Ray: "Yeah, I thought about coming myself but didn't want to cramp your style. Always preferred 90s stuff too; Prodigy, Chemical Brothers."

Jordan: "That's why it was so busy! I'd tried to keep this one pretty quiet."

Becky: "You shouldn't put them on when we are struggling."

Jordan stared daggers at her and was thankful Gwawr and Ray didn't say anything but Jordan hated what they might be thinking. It wasn't as if they could help him financially, he'd rather top himself than take help in that way.

Jordan: "We aren't struggling Becky, I've got some stuff lined up for the next few months."

He didn't actually have much lined up over the next few

months and the things that he had, he wasn't looking forward to.

Ray: "Well, the people who went from my work said it was a cracking night."

Jordan: "That's a silver lining. It was pretty epic this one, the amp didn't work so the music didn't kick off until gone midnight, but there were a lot of people who came up expecting it."

Jordan didn't mention the dead-looking guy; it seemed bad enough they knew he'd set up a party.

Becky spoke again, much to Jordan's annoyance.

Becky: "Why do you like these parties? They just sound like they tire you out for the whole week?"

Jordan: "People love the music and the social. It feels great dancing with a load of friends and it can feel a bit otherworldly. It's a blow out for some people from the everyday mundane. The joy of dance, music and connection for some, oblivion for others. I know of few feelings like it to be honest. It's worth being tired for a few days afterwards from my perspective."

The rest of the conversation for the evening was lost on Jordan who was pissed at Becky and was busy contemplating shit like bills, his infrequent and badly paid work, and little else.

Then his Golf started to go in and out of the garage. Having some problems, the garage struggled to fix it and it became a very unreliable vehicle. But he couldn't afford another, He'd drawn as much cash out as he could on credit cards and his options seemed limited. He remembered Eleri telling him about her car epic when she was skint and felt a strong sense of empathy toward his sister.

With no cash the options of what Becky and he could do also felt pretty dismal. She wasn't into walking or climbing and it seemed to Jordan that they just spent their time together stressed about having no money. He started to avoid any social situations which might lead to financially embarrassing situations, as there had been a few and for Jordan this was a few too many.

One day, having a rest on a walk through the slate quarries on his own, he sat in one of the small quarry blast shelters as the rain washed across the small door. He smoked and brooded on his dismal last few months and lack of any future prospects. Christ, he felt depressed, about his quarrels with Becky, about his lack of work, about his fucked car and about the fucking constant rain. He could split up with Becky but then he'd just be alone with his other problems and whether he loved her or not, he knew he was lucky she could put up with him. He doubted anyone else could.

He looked at the chasm only a few metres away from where he sat in his shelter. The chasm was hundreds of feet deep and if he chose he could just take a few steps and end all his worries there and then. He felt so detached about everything, not looking forward to anything and the idea of going back home to worry with Becky about bills seemed less appealing than taking the plunge.

He edged out into the rain and neared the drop so he had only one step to go over the precipice. He looked down into it, his rollie he'd been smoking had gone out as the rain drowned it. Jordan cursed, he couldn't even have a last few puffs he thought. Staring into the pit he remembered he was going to see Eleri in a couple of days. He moved back from the edge and back into the shelter to try and get another rollie together. He remembered a time when he felt relatively happy, certainly by comparison to this, back when he had some job security and his self-esteem had felt a lot higher. As he looked out at the rain and the chasm, he just felt lost.

*

It was at least nice to catch up with Eleri one morning. They went for a walk around the lake together, via a couple of ciggy breaks sat in the sun on one of the many round rocks that protruded into the lake on the far side. They'd not managed to catch up for a while with Eleri working away a fair bit. Jordan had been glad of this as he didn't want her to know how much he was struggling.

Jordan: "How's work going? Good effort getting a job at the Uni."

Eleri: "Pretty good thanks, better paid than the contract stuff I was doing and less travel. I was getting a bit tired of moving around before and it's nice to be back again."

Jordan: "It's good that you'll be back soon. Have you seen Jacob at all?"

Eleri: "We don't speak to each other now, bit too painful. I messed him around after we split up."

Jordan could see pain in Eleri's eyes and changed the subject.

Jordan: "You were missed at the last party."

Eleri: "I know, gutted, I was moving the last of my stuff up from Birmingham and couldn't face starting to lecture with a come down either. I've got to choose my nights nowadays. It sounded pretty wild, good effort again. How are you enjoying freelance work? Sorry you lost the full-time job."

Jordan: "It's ok thanks. I need to be a bit more organised, remember to invoice and double check I've been paid, more calls to people too."

Eleri: "Sounds ok, at least it will have more variety. How's Becky doing, she still at the Vic? I should know this, sorry I've been slack with keeping in touch the last few months. I'll be moving into Llanberis soon so will be around loads more. You know what it's like when you've been living out of your car."

Jordan: "No worries, you've had a ton on. Becky is ok, not been getting on as well as we have done though. I find her a little boring and we've been ratty with each other."

Eleri: "Might be worth having a holiday or some time out. It can be tough when you're living with someone for a long time."

Jordan: "Some time out might well be the option. A lot of time out."

Eleri: "Ha, don't be miserable little J. Becky is really nice."

Jordan: "Guess so, but it doesn't matter how nice someone is if things just aren't clicking. I don't feel as comfortable around her now, bit more estranged."

Eleri: "Mum said you were having some issues with your car? Christ I had an epic with that Escort, hope it's not as tragic as that."

Jordan: "I could definitely do without it. What did the Stoics say? 'Amor Fati', a love of fate, loving everything that happens. I'm struggling to see what there is to love about a fucked car."

Eleri: "Fucking Stoics could be full of shit little bro, doubt they ever had the stress of a screwed vehicle. Let me know if you need a hand with it. You can use my car when I'm back in town next month. I only need to get into Bangor, so can get the bus or a ride in with friends."

They walked on to the village and Jordan gave Eleri a strong hug which lasted a while.

Jordan: "Goodbye Eleri."

Eleri: "You ok Jordan? We'll catch up soon, let's do dinner at mine next week."

Jordan: "I'm ok, thanks. Dinner sounds top."

Jordan waved as they parted company. He felt enveloped in darkness.

*

He'd given suicide a bit of thought over the years, and since he'd lost the security of his full-time job the thought had become more regular. Bertrand Russell had written that good nature was the result of ease and security, not of an arduous life of struggle, and Jordan felt his nature had gotten worse and worse. But the fact was none of the possible methods of exits was appealing.

Hanging, suffocating from car exhaust, drowning, overdose and even a jump off a cliff can all be done wrong and might end up leaving you maimed and even more depressed. One of the more appealing ways Jordan had thought about was to go into the mountains and try to get exposure, but the winters were too mild in Wales. Perhaps in Scotland he'd get away with it but he would prefer to exit the world in an area he knew well.

He felt a failure and he wasn't looking forward to anything. He didn't want to hang out with Becky but neither did he want the trauma of breaking up with her, nor did he imagine someone else would make him happy. Work was boring as hell and paid little, and he saw his prospects of life improvement as minus 1000. He'd read something on the NHS website related to depression but he do very much doubted the NHS could sort him out a job, money and a value-driven life. He'd felt at rock bottom for over a year and he felt out of options. Destitution beckoned to him, the awful gaping maw which was waiting in the wings for many millions of piss poor people who got unlucky or made unwise decisions.

So, one evening in late October, he found himself walking up Yr Wyddfa to above a cliff famous to rock climbers, Clogwyn Du'r Arddu, which translated to the black cliff of darkness. He'd climbed on the slab in the middle a couple of years before and had done a climb called Longlands. The harder climbs were where he hiked above and sat down though, high above Great Wall and the Indian Face. He was wearing blue denim jeans and a green Nepalese jumper Eleri had gotten him. He'd hardly taken it off for the last few weeks. He'd finally settled on the best possible method for committing suicide.

In his pocket he had a fair-sized bag of MDMA and a packet of tobacco, both had been given to him by Jacob who'd clocked that he was skint. The cliff he sat above was about 200 feet high with a rocky landing, and it was unlikely to fail. He'd thought about doing it in one of the big holes in the slate quarry, but he didn't have quite the affinity for the quarries as Eleri did. She loved the place. Jordan did like Yr Wyddfa though. His dad had told him bedtime stories about dragons living beneath this cliff, in the lake, Llyn Du'r Arddu. He felt he was lucky to be able to choose somewhere special to him to disappear when his life choices all seemed otherwise dimly lit.

Wetting his little finger, Jordan proceeded to dab the MDMA and washed it down with some posh ciders he'd brought up that he'd nicked from the Spar. Then he lit a rollie, holding it to his mouth with his nicotine-stained fingers. He had a Walkman on him, playing his favourite Queen songs, one of his few soft spots, music-wise, outside of techno.

A bit over an hour later his pupils were fully dilated, and a warm feeling suffused his body. He'd been caning rollies almost as fast as he could roll and smoke them. He looked at the fern moss his hand had grasped, one of his dad's favourites. He whispered, "sorry mam," and with the weight of regrets for deeds done, and not done, he threw himself off the cliff.

His world stopped.

CHAPTER 9:
GALAR (GRIEF)

The world stopped in reality for Jordan and was soon to end metaphorically for Gwawr.

She'd been gutted when Becky had mentioned her and Jordan were struggling and she'd been thinking about what she might sell to help them out and how to do it without letting Jordan know, perhaps giving something to Becky. Blokes could be stubborn dickheads.

With these thoughts in mind, a knock at the door brought her to opening it and seeing the unusual sight of two police officers, a man and a woman.

She welcomed them in, wondering why they were there. Once they were sat down, she felt detached from her body as they delivered the news and all she could hear was her heart trying to beat itself out of her chest. Her head felt like needles had been driven into it on all sides and she didn't recognise the wailing voice which came out of her mouth.

Ray and Megan joined Gwawr in the living room at some point, but Gwawr was still outside her body somewhere thinking about Jordan, as a baby, a toddler, having to stop him taking every machine apart he could get his hands on, the feeling of pride when he was getting his qualifications.

He'd often seemed a bit moody but she couldn't believe he was that unhappy. Every interaction she'd had with him in recent years went through her mind. What should she have done differently? How could she have helped him? Eventually feeling an overpowering claustrophobia she left the house and ran as fast as she could up towards Elidir Fawr. Slowing to a trot as the mountain steepened, she continued up in constant tears and, on reaching the top, cried into the grey clouds, wind and rain:

"Pam? Pam!?"

The wind on the top was bitter and combined with occasional heavy rain it made it feel truly cold. But these elements didn't touch Gwawr's awareness at all. After hours of shivering and crying on the top, Ray and Eleri eventually found her, the pair looking like ghosts coming out of the clouds towards her. They wrapped a blanket around her mildly hypothermic body and cradled her in their arms before making their way back down to their house and memories.

Gwawr struggled to sleep for days, with exhaustion being the only avenue allowing rest, and she certainly couldn't eat. Mind reeling constantly, her normal strong will felt broken.

Becky came and stayed with them, feeling alone in the house in Llanberis with too many memories.

The next few days Gwawr spent much of her time looking at pictures and wondering what she could have done. Cards came in from neighbours, but Gwawr could take no solace in their pity. After a few days of feeling exhausted and oblivious to time, she remembered Eleri coming to see her in the garden and putting her hands on Gwawr's back.

Eleri: "Mum, you need to eat."

Gwawr: "What could I have done Eleri?"

Eleri: "You couldn't have done anything mam. I was close with Jordan; I didn't realise either."

Gwawr: "He was so young Eleri. He could have had a family, he could have been happy!"

Eleri: "Please eat something mum, for me, please?"

Eleri brought Gwawr inside and watched her with concern as she managed to have some cawl (soup), her first food for a week. She looked haggard. Eleri felt totally fucked herself but during her time working with hard up families she'd learnt a bit about dealing with people in trauma, giving them compassion, acknowledging what had happened. She knew she shouldn't be surprised or alarmed at the intensity of feeling but her mum seemed totally destroyed, like her soul had been sucked out of her, and Eleri felt powerfully screwed herself.

Ray seemed in better shape than Gwawr, and Eleri and Megan did what they could to help organise the funeral and to notify friends and relatives. Thomas was around, leg seeming even more lame than usual, smoking even more heavily than usual and looking in as deep a state of grief as anyone but Gwawr. Gwawr seemed alone and isolated, whatever anyone tried to offer emotional support. Eleri was thankful when Becky went back to her parents' house again as she'd started to struggle with dealing with so much grief. There was enough to be found within her close family, which felt like a black hole with Gwawr at the centre.

The funeral day came, in Bangor, overlooking the sea, with some friends reciting some memories of their time with Jordan. The weather was dreich, raining and blustery.

Gwawr was hardly there, an empty shell. She had nothing she could offer on this day. Eleri also felt fucked and detached, with everything that had occurred seeming surreal. Megan and Ray were more tearful than Eleri. She felt such a deep regret at not having noticed that Jordan needed help that she'd have much preferred to cut off one of her limbs if it would give her the chance to go back in time. Profound regret.

Zoe and Isabelle were there, next to Eleri, lending support. Zoe looked almost as broken as Becky. Thomas, his broad shoulders staying near to Ray's and his eyes downcast, thinking of the small child he used to throw into the air. His nicotine-stained fingers wiped tears from his face, one hand holding onto Ray, the other holding a cigarette.

Eleri was surprised to see Smiler there. She hadn't realised he knew Jordan but she was glad he'd made the effort to come, with his downturned face of pain fitting the mood well. There must have been over 200 people who came to give their regards, including Mushroom Bob, various people related to Blue Peris, the outdoor community, the party scene and general Llanberis locals. It did warm Eleri's heart a bit by seeing Osian there, with his mum Elliw and father Glyn. It had been some time since she'd caught up with him or his parents.

On the walls of the funeral parlour there were lots of different pictures of Jordan that friends had given, and a few Eleri and Megan had put together. Eleri had put the one up Osian had given her with Jordan between Zoe and Eleri after she'd rescued him from drowning in Dali's Hole. Ray had insisted on playing Guns N' Roses 'Sweet Child O' Mine'. To be fair Jordan had liked it, guess it was what he was brought up on as Ray had played it all the time. Eleri knew that Jordan would have preferred to be cremated and have his ashes blasted out of big speakers playing techno in a cool spot but she didn't express this view to her parents, so burial in Bangor it was. Before they all dispersed, Eleri lay the slate plaque Osian had made with Jordan's name engraved in it on his grave.

*

The months passed and Gwawr remembered slipping from reality, it was a fine thing to be able to escape. This must have been what Jordan wanted to do at his parties. She heard voices occasionally but they sounded distant.

Megan: "Mum you have to stop this, please."

Ray's voice sounded panicked:

"You need help Gwawr, you need help."

She didn't remember when she'd left her house to live somewhere else for a while. She felt so confused. Gwawr couldn't tell how much time had passed when Eleri came in to see her.

Eleri: "Nice to see you mum, you're looking well."

Gwawr: "What could we have done Eleri?"

Eleri didn't know.

*

After a few months of struggling Gwawr ceased to talk altogether, but at least was deemed able to return home. Struggling was perhaps an understatement. She would rarely leave the house. Ray looked after her as best he could. Eleri and Megan helped as much as possible, and Megan seemed most adept at handling the situation, perhaps from her time working in a care home when she was younger.

Thomas would often come round and sit with Gwawr and chat with Ray and smoke. He even started to make his own cawl to bring for Gwawr. Ray had never smoked before but started to join Thomas, feeling the need to do something other than talk. If Gwawr had been able to talk when Eleri was there she knew she would have given Thomas and Ray a mouthful as the air in the living room seemed ripe even to Eleri who smoked a few each day.

The name Gwawr meant dawn. It was looking like a bleak fucking dawn to Eleri though, and it looked like they'd lost more than just her little brother when he jumped off that fucking cliff.

CHAPTER 10: Y DAILEN (THE LEAVES)

The transporter van felt pretty full with Ug, Nodder, Jon and Lewis in it, but it may have just been the skunk that permeated the air in the van as Jon drove them down the Llŷn Peninsula to go climbing. Ug and Nodder were big, broad guys, both with fair hair and with Ug suiting his name. Jon was smaller but still pretty ripped, making Lewis the runt of the group and the youngest by a good few years. Ug was apparently less like a human oak tree once, but then he got a job on the Millennium Dome drilling metre-long holes in it for months and he bulked out considerably. Combined with years of building work afterwards, this made him one of the physically strongest people Lewis knew.

Lewis liked the odd spliff but was pretty blown away by the older guy's consistency. Before one spliff was finished, Ug had his huge jar of skunk open and another was made to take its place and passed around. Once they were parked up they walked down a small lush valley next to a stream, past old Manganese quarries nestled into the sidewalls. This led them to the boulders on the beach at Porth Ysgo, a very scenic place to go bouldering. The three older men didn't slow down on the spliffs and Lewis was impressed that it didn't seem to impede their ability to climb too much. It was a great spot next to the sea, with some of the boulders even requiring a low tide to access them. The weather was often considerably better than in the mountains, not suffering from the relief rainfall, and on this day the sun shone down brightly.

It was Nodder's 40th birthday, but much of the talk was morbid, contrasting the brightness of the day.

Jon: "Fucking poor Jordan, I didn't see that coming. He was young, eh."

Lewis thought Jon was right; none of them had seen it coming. It's not something you expect anyone to do. It seemed almost unnatural.

Ug sat on a rock in the sun, a tight white t-shirt on, biceps bulging, threatening to rip it like the Hulk. He puffed out some smoke.

Ug: "Grim and tragic. How is Eleri, Lewis?"

Lewis: "Eleri seems pretty introverted but obviously devastated, they were very close. Her mum, Gwawr, is pretty fucked. Think she needs some serious help."

Nodder: "There is nothing worse in the world I think for a mother to lose a son. It's gotta shake people's world to the core."

Jon: "Did he leave a note? Anyone know why? He did seem pretty into parties, too much MDMA and bad come downs can screw with your mind. I meant to catch up with him, just been wrapped up in my own shit. It can be hard hanging out with people when they are properly down too, often haven't got a good word to say about anyone. Not that Jordan seemed like that."

Lewis: "No note. I get the vibe off people I've spoken to, including Eleri, that things deteriorated a lot when he lost his job. I think he was struggling financially, and suffered with depression now and then too."

Ug: "It can be well stressful being skint. He could have done some work with me; he used to do some building stuff in the past."

Jon: "I guess their family is pretty skint, eh. I was going out with someone once who was from a pretty wealthy background and expected me to pay for everything. I had to explain to them that if they got into trouble their family would be able to look after them financially, whereas my family have zero and if I got injured and couldn't work I'd be fucked. One close family member got into some trouble with debt and I was helping them out as much as I could. My girlfriend was pretty clueless about it, just didn't seem to get it. We split up eventually obvs."

Nodder: "He should have looked into rope access work. I know loads of people doing well out of that."

Ug: "It's not always that great to be honest but, yeah, he could have earned an ok wage pretty quickly. It involves working away from home a lot though. The financial crash has hit that too, a lot of it is construction related and it has been hit hard, similar to the outdoor sector getting nailed I guess. For a lot of the city crew or people in power the outdoors is a want rather than a need, so it's easy for them to sting it with cuts."

Lewis felt fortunate that he had a job. After finishing a course in environmental conservation he did an apprenticeship scheme which allowed him to become a warden on the Carneddau, the eastern mountain range in Snowdonia, an area he now knew very well. Small semi-wild ponies roamed much of it, and an orange coloured one with a blonde mane was his favourite of the bunch. His friend Maisy had made a great painting of it, with the Ogwen Valley and Penrhyn slate quarry behind.

Getting a normal job had meant he'd pretty much stopped drug dealing which had been his main income for a number of years. He only got enough for himself and a couple of friends nowadays. It was a lot less stressful; some of the people you had to deal with could be a bit gnarly and a lot of people you were flogging the gear to were nervous about getting ripped off or the gear being duff. He'd never been cut out to be a salesman.

It had been a close-run thing with his normal job. He'd had a couple of dickhead bosses he'd really had to hold his anger in check for. There was one guy at a similar level to Lewis who was a huge coaster, but had got a promotion and lorded it over Lewis. Given his new power, he even threatened not to give Lewis the holiday he'd asked for on their first meeting after the promotion. Lewis was gobsmacked as for years it had seemed the guy was permanently on holiday and did almost no work when he was around. There was even a point where Lewis and some colleagues were actually going to buy the guy a giant mug coaster as a joke. Thankfully he eventually transferred so Lewis didn't have to put up with the little Hitler anymore. Eleri had said power can go to people's heads and she wasn't wrong. People couldn't work hard for those they didn't respect.

Lewis: "Eleri said Jordan had had enough of labouring and building work. It sounded pretty tough the work he was doing, a bit dangerous too. I think he electrocuted himself once, got blown across a room - the sparky had told him the electric was fully off and he sawed through a live wire!"

Ug: "It can shaft your body for sure, I know a few lads in the trade who have stuffed their backs and then struggle to work. I nearly took my face off with the kick back off a circular saw once too. You've got to be very careful."

Jon: "It's bloody hard for young people to find something worthwhile and meaningful to do work wise nowadays. It's all super insecure too, zero-hour contract bollocks. Have you seen 'Sorry We Missed You'? It's a Ken Loach film and says a lot about modern work."

Lewis: "Nobody knows that better than Eleri. She would have helped Jordan if she'd had an inkling he was in trouble. Guess she has been away a fair bit so didn't clock his work situation so much."

Jon: "Let us know if we can help at all and pass on our regards when you see her."

Lewis: "Will do, I'll hopefully catch her next week for a climb or a beer."

Jon: "Where's Osian? Did he not fancy it today?"

Lewis: "He's well into his work atm. He's in his workshop loads working on different rocks and metals. He's gotten really good, made a dragon out of granite half the size of me. He's selling some of his work in galleries in Caernarfon and Bangor too. I'm chuffed for him!"

Jon: "At least someone has found something they're into. Good for Osian."

Lewis: "Think he's worried about Eleri too. He's always had a proper soft spot for her."

Ug: "I can see why! Lovely, smart and into parties too."

Nodder: "Top effort with *your* work too Lewis, enjoy it while you can. Your 20s are spent having fun drinking, partying and having sex, your 30s having kids and work stress, then in your 40s you go to counselling for what went on in the two decades prior. From then on it's mainly funerals in the diary between personal health scares."

Ug: "Happy birthday mate, you miserable bastard."

Nodder: "Unfortunately an element of truth there though. I spoke to a friend, James, who was a professional climber. He said he went to counselling with his partner and she told him and the counsellor she hadn't realised how into climbing he was!"

They all snickered at this.

Jon: "How is your love life Lewis? You going out with Bryony?"

Lewis had just started to see Bryony, who was someone with fairly similar interests to him outside of getting baked, and someone he'd clicked with pretty quickly. It was early days yet though.

Lewis blushed a little: "Hadn't realised anyone knew about us! Yeah we've been hanging out a little bit, I really like her. She cooks a killer quiche too."

Jon: "Yeah, good catch there Lewis, she's sound."

Nodder: "Enjoy it while you can! You've got the love chemicals working in the first year; dopamine, oxytocin, serotonin... then when they wear off, you'll start looking at things that piss you off about that person. I don't know how humans maintain long term relationships."

Jon and Ug looked at each other and shook their heads.

Jon: "A fountain of positivity as ever Nodder. People adapt, or split up, and if they don't adapt but stay together, they often end up as miserable sods nobody wants to hang out with. I know a ton of couples who would have been better off splitting up. I guess for some people bad company is better than no company. If you've been in a relationship for a while it can feel pretty lonely rattling around a house by yourself."

Nodder: "Yeah, I found it hard once. It was just me and the sound of the rats in the attic. I was worried they'd just find my skeleton after the rats had finished me off, a lonely end indeed."

After the daylight started to fade they headed back to the van, spliffs still getting passed between them, but plenty left in Ug's jar.

Lewis saw some rust-coloured autumnal oak leaves blowing about on the path on the way back up and felt that it resembled people's lives quite well. There was only so much say someone had in their lives, however strong minded they were, and people were left to the winds of chance that made up their fate.

What work people ended up doing, who they went out with, what hobbies they had... so much chance decides these things. Lewis thought about points in his life where it could have forked completely; he could be in jail for dealing drugs; could have died on a rockface, lying at the bottom, rather than just having a 'close call'; he could be still with Zoe rather than Bryony...but to be fair he was pretty baked and these were flying thoughts in the space of a few seconds. If a few things had gone differently for Jordan he could have still been here and in good spirits perhaps. Who knows?

They headed back to the Vaynol Arms and played pool and necked a few more pints to celebrate Nodder's 40th. Lewis was glad they didn't go back to one of their houses to get more baked or it would have been a rough start to the week ahead.

*

Waking up in his flat in Llanberis the next day, Lewis' head was still pretty banging and he swore to take it much easier on the booze from then on. He couldn't remember how he got home either. He eventually went on his Facebook and some 'memories' popped up on it, pictures from only two years ago, at Jordan's house, a load of them hanging out after being out to Hendre for Fright Night. Amazing how happiness could change to tragedy in a short space of time. Lewis had known a few people who had got hit by shit luck which changed their lives for the worse.

People who had crashed a vehicle, writing it off and being unable to afford another, which affected their ability to get a job. One guy, Jim, would hardly leave the house since his wife left ten years ago, heartbroken and having lost interest in life. People who had been sacked and had then turned to booze to drown their sorrows, making them even more skint. Lewis had recently seen in the local newspaper an obituary to a guy he went to primary school with, Matthew Vasquez, found drowned near Caernarfon. There were no other details given, but Lewis remembered Matthew had trouble with him of various kinds from a young age. Lewis hadn't told Eleri yet. She had plenty of other shit to deal with at the moment and didn't need Lewis adding to it with crap news.

But Jordan was the only person Lewis had known fairly well and had hung out with who had ended their life. Lewis thought it must have taken a lot of bottle and that Jordan must have given it a lot of thought to go as far as it's possible to go. To the very end.

Lewis had climbed on Clogwyn Du'r Arddu a few times, his favourite climb being A Midsummer Night's Dream, starting very near where Jordan had landed. Lewis' friends in the rescue team had said he would have died instantly and for that Lewis was grateful. He couldn't think of a nice way of dying, but swiftly was as good as it gets.

He messaged Eleri on Facebook.

L: *Hey Eleri, hope you are doing ok. Fancy getting out Wednesday night? I'll give you a belay and we can go for a pint in the Heights afterwards. Cheers, Lewis*

He heard nothing back and figured she was still spending time with her family or was possibly away working. Her presence had been pretty ephemeral the last few years. He messaged Osian too, being more nervous about checking in on his friends to make sure they were ok since losing Jordan.

L: *Hey Osian, you about this week? Fancy getting out in Llanberis pass?*

O: *Sounds good, Tuesday? I can be at yours at 3pm*

L: *Ace, see you then. Any word from Eleri? I dropped her a line about Wednesday night but I haven't heard back*

O: *Nothing for a while. Let me know if you get out with her Wednesday*

L: *Sound, will do, have a good wknd*

Lewis felt fortunate to have people like Osian and Eleri as friends who had been close for many years and was proud of them both for what they had achieved. Osian finding fulfilment in creativity and making a living through it, and Eleri doing what she'd always said she wanted to do; trying to make the world a fairer place. Lewis hoped the trauma Eleri had suffered wasn't going to change her too much. Sometimes trauma could really change people. He knew that sometimes a tragedy in people's lives could undo them.

He made a coffee, rolled and lit up a spliff and turned the news on. None of it was good. There really were a total bunch of lying no-good crooks in government at the moment. He didn't know how they got any sleep or why they bothered to do the things they did. Why would you turn up to or even desire a job you were clearly absolutely crap at and seemingly intentionally make millions of people's lives worse? After a couple of tokes he turned the news back off. The world was definitely a better place when you were ignorant to what was going on, and when the current people in charge talked, it all sounded like complete bollocks and gobbledygook to Lewis. Posh twats too.

Many of the people in charge were leaves that had been blown through a load of complete shit. He wondered idly if this was one of the points Jordan had thought about that had made him depressed. Lewis thought it would make any sane person pretty depressed. He put the crap, divisive, inept leaders to the back of his mind and enjoyed the joint and coffee.

CHAPTER 11:
CASAU (HATE)

Eleri had never really felt true hatred but in the years that followed her little brother's death it slowly built up. She felt changes developing within her, big changes, the kind that allow people to go as far as it's possible to go, places most people rightly have boundaries preventing themselves from going. Eleri knew that grief has no timeframe; it could be unpredictable and alarm people with its intensity, but as the years wore on, she could feel it like a lead weight in her head, building. And next to the grief there was a powerful hate.

Throughout the months following his death, Eleri realised that she'd totally missed how skint Jordan had been. She had just thought Jordan and Becky were careful. However, Eleri had spoken with Becky when she was back living in the area and also talked to some of Jordan's closest friends. She looked back on the times they'd met up in the months prior to his death, only doing things that were cost-free; not eating in cafes, only wanting to go for walks, bumming some tobacco from Jacob. How did she miss it?

She was absolutely gutted to discover this was a big factor in his deterioration, one she could have helped with if she'd been observant. Why didn't he tell her? Of course she now knew that he was ashamed... who wants people to know that they're struggling? She'd been putting money into some fucking environmental company, thinking she was doing a good deed to help future generations. If she'd known about Jordan she'd have been able to give him and Becky the money instead. She could have helped give him some positive direction like she had when he was younger and struggling with his labouring work.

The final straw for Eleri turned out to be a funny thing. Sat in her living room on Goodman Street in Llanberis one miserable winters evening, she was simply watching The Laundromat, starring Meryl Streep, Gary Oldman, and Antonio Banderas, laying out how corrupt offshore accounts were. And there they were, some of the main culprits of austerity shown at the end of the movie, having had their riches stashed away in Panama, untaxed, in shell companies, clearly loaded beyond imagination and pushing a narrative which had helped finish off her brother.

She stared at the screen and was close to destroying the TV for a few minutes, eyes narrowed to slits and knuckles tightened as hard as she could, thinking about smashing their faces with a plant pot, for much good breaking her TV would do for her or her dead brother.

She thought about the causes of the banking crisis and she looked at the solution people had put out there for it. It was caused by bankers and lack of regulations, but the little people had to pay for it through cuts, as well as reduced services and life opportunities. This was an area Eleri had some expertise in, having spent much of her life studying wealth inequalities, usually on more of a local and national scale. Destroyed services, destroyed jobs, destroyed lives. The lives of her brother and, as a knock-on effect, her family. And who had pushed this dangerous narrative but the super-rich, those born never to know the worry of not being able to pay for necessities.

Eleri watched The Big Short again and again, making notes on who and what created the crash. It appeared that bankers insured trillions in risky derivatives, leading to a global economic crisis and then got bailed out by taxpayers before carrying on what they were doing before the crash with no accountability. The people in power were very much the buddies of the bankers.

She watched The Laundromat again, making notes on the people involved with offshore accounts and those who had pushed austerity. People with vast wealth who had destroyed so many lives through their dangerous ideology. If Jordan hadn't lost his job he might well still be with them. Even in the early mornings, when she first woke up, her blood was often boiling thinking about it.

She knew the UK, like the US, had a steep inequality gradient, i.e., quite a few very, very rich people holding far too much wealth and at the opposite end of the spectrum a shit ton of people with debt and serious life problems, but she hadn't realised quite how criminal it all was. Too much money for the bastards at the top who were stripping away the safety net for those at the bottom, screwing the NHS, blaming vulnerable benefit claimants and constantly fibbing that there was no money. The hate that had started to permeate Eleri's mind felt like it was coursing through her bloodstream and affecting her whole body.

It started to feel like waves pressing on her mind, pounding it, and needing a vent somehow. Eleri had maintained her climbing over the years. She liked how it gives you a clear focus, how nothing else matters in the world except the next move to gain height. She was proud of some of the climbs she had done with friends, routes such as Central Sadness, A Midsummer Night's Dream and The Long Run were all big leads which required a very good head, a thoughtful approach and the respect of even the best climbers. Her friends trusted her climbing skills and regarded her as a safe pair of hands to be on a rockface with. You didn't want to be on a long climb wondering if your partner had built an anchor or belay incorrectly.

She'd only ever climbed without a rope a few times, mainly on easy routes with friends nearby doing the same thing. It's referred to as soloing and the consequences of a fall are clear;

you hit the ground and are likely to be killed or seriously injured and therefore cannot afford to fall.

The waves which had started pressing on her mind needed satiating somehow and so Eleri soon found herself in the large slate hole called California, alone, and looking at one of the hardest climbs she'd done, Central Sadness, graded E5 6a. It went up a central fault line in a 150-foot sheer face of slate. It was thin and technical at first, then petered out into slate shelves through steeper terrain before opening up into a fairly deep crack at 80 feet which you could get your fingers inside but still full of lots of tricky moves for even a good climber. Eleri had never heard of anyone trying this climb without a rope.

Eleri's whole body felt full of heat and she knew she wasn't thinking straight. Instead, she was full more of a powerful impulse to take a huge risk, to face oblivion. She surprised herself with how calm she was with the anger and grief which was radiating from her body and mind, channelling it into a cold determination.

She tightened her rock shoes and made sure they were clean, put her chalk bag around her waist, stretched to touch her toes a couple of times to limber up, took a couple of deep breaths, and set off.

She flowed up the first few metres which were tricky, but not far from the ground, then at eight metres she rested on a ledge. From here on upwards a fall would mean serious injury or death, with the sharp jumbled slate bottom giving little mirth to a falling climber.

Adjusting her glasses, Eleri re-chalked and set off determinedly, quickly but with precise foot and hand placements, arriving at a ledge where most climbers belay and rest before continuing.

She set herself, chalked again and took control of her breathing, taking deep steady breaths. The first section of the climb had felt much easier than when she'd had a rope on with the added adrenaline coursing through her veins.

Keeping herself steady she made rockovers up big edges and jugs to gain the main crack forming the upper part of the climb. From here, Eleri concentrated and pushed her body and mind through each hard crux section assuredly until near the last hard move when she could see easy climbing only a couple of metres above. Suddenly the wave of grief, hate and energy that was in her earlier faded away and the realisation dawned on her that she'd done little soloing and was 130 feet up and sure to die if she fucked up the next insecure move. As the wave receded, so did the calmness she'd managed to channel from it.

A terrible moment or two transpired, something which can kill a solo climber as easy as a loose rock or slip began to set in...panic. As it started to pierce Eleri's mind she pulled herself closer to the rockface on finger holds, arms suddenly feeling very tired and unable to focus on the moves that could take her to the easier climbing and safety that lay just above her position. Her stomach tightened and she started to breathe crazily fast. Sweat began to drip off her forehead onto her glasses, not improving her situation. After a few dreadful minutes where Eleri had flashbacks to memorable bits of her life, meeting Jacob, Osian's slate present, saving Jordan, the moon over Llyn Padarn one night with friends... dozens of memories... the hate then fed back in and she took the emotion and used it to cut clean through the panic.

She knew she had to do something fast before her energy faded. Regaining her poise she peered down through her sweaty glasses for the best foot options. She shook out each hand with chalk to dry them from sweat and, breathing hard, she sprung onto the footholds allowing her left hand to slap a big flat handhold above. Her right hand joined it and the panic fully receded, replaced with elation as she scampered up the easier terrain to the top and lay on her back for a minute staring at the clouds in the sky.

She'd just soloed a route as hard as any she'd done with a rope before. She pushed herself up and looked down into the hundreds of feet of void in the hole from which she'd risen. She couldn't believe what she'd just done. Before setting off it had felt like the weight of the world was pressing down on her mind, leading to her to setting off on the climb. The death of her brother, her mother giving up, the toffs screwing the poor and laughing with their money in profoundly corrupt tax havens.

"Am I losing it?!" she cried out loud into the cool evening breeze which had picked up. She didn't particularly care if she was losing it. The overwhelming negative feelings she'd channelled at the start had dissipated and contrasted with the feeling of being alive that she now had at the top. The sun was going down behind Anglesey. Eleri had dealt with this wave in a very questionable manner but she could already feel the start of a much bigger wave building. She meandered her way out of the slate heaps back to where she'd parked in Bus Stop Quarry.

The man who had been watching her ascent with great concern made his way down out of the quarry. He'd found it awful to watch as soloing is by and large an unnatural thing to spectate upon. He could see there was something up with Eleri. He'd been ready to call for help but didn't want to put her off by calling. He doubted there was anyone nearby anyway. As he puffed on his rollie he decided he'd keep a closer eye on Eleri in the near future.

*

After her experience on Central Sadness Eleri cooled off for a bit, but started going onto social media, particularly twitter, for news and also to air some of her views on austerity, Brexit and Trump amongst other topics. She'd often have discussions and arguments with people she didn't know at all. She went for some of the senior Tories online, some of whom had promoted climate change denial, and those that had loads of money off in Panama but had the gall to push austerity.

She had one spat with a particular fantasist, a gullible type who sucked up much of the bullshit the papers put out regardless of evidence. He didn't like being told publicly that Eleri thought he was a moron. After their altercation he said he would send a complaint into the university Eleri worked at and, to be fair, the moron followed through on his promise.

On the way into the University the next day a friend of Eleri's called Tom who had been following the online argument messaged her. He was something of a bright spark on the internet. He said he'd looked at the profile of the character she'd interacted with and said he wasn't harmless and had a history of entrapment, trying to provoke people and trying to get people sacked who he disagreed with.

Tom: "You can check his social media account by putting it into any of the analytics. It shows that most of his interactions are awful, and he also tags himself into any interaction in case you block him."

When she had a break for lunch, she got a call to go to the Vice Chancellor's office, Professor Edward Hughes. She'd always got on well with him in their brief conversations.

He smiled as she walked in and got straight into it.

Edward: "Hi Eleri. I hope you are well, and I am sorry to ask you in here. We received quite the complaint email this morning."

He pushed a printed version of it towards Eleri. Eleri skimmed down the four pages. Her friend Tom was right, the card had tagged himself into posts so he could screengrab for use in complaints he made.

Eleri: "I'm happy to contest every point he makes, Edward. This character also has a history of complaining to organisations for any person he doesn't like, as well as trying to organise horrible online pile-ons for people he argues with. He's got plenty of other deluded online friends who hang out on forums together."

Eleri showed Edward the messages her friend Tom had given her.

Edward: "I will handle this. The man comes across as having a screw loose, but we need to be seen to follow up and to have a record of having dealt with things like this. Please be careful on social media Eleri, the world is very different to what it was ten years ago. Nowadays anyone can ruin their reputation in a few seconds with the wrong post after a glass of wine or two on an evening. If I say the wrong thing it could easily threaten my position, that's why I prefer to stay away from all social media. Some of the people I know have views I disagree with strongly."

Eleri: "I understand Edward, and thanks for your support on this. I'll stay off social media for a while and sort my privacy settings out too."

Edward: "Thank you Eleri. You are doing some great work; there is lots of excellent feedback on your lectures. If I were you I'd focus on that. Some people I know seem to waste half their lives having arguments online with people they don't even know!"

Eleri waved goodbye and thought Edward had made a good point.

*

Eleri carried on with life as normal for a while. She was lecturing on modules she herself had once sat in on; economics, politics and community development.

When teaching a first year group in one of the large lecture theatres in the sandstone Main Arts building, her thoughts on the toxic politics started to come out into her teaching.

Eleri: "Can anyone name the type of politics which has grown rife in the last few years?"

A smallish fair-haired student, Emma, put her hand up: "It's populism."

Eleri: "Correct."

Eleri wrote populism on the white board and put a bubble around it.

Eleri: "What does this mean?"

Various students shouted out words Eleri put around the bubble. Division, heated rhetoric, blame, people versus elite, demagogy, over-simplistic answers, opportunism, emotions, hate, Nazis, Trump.

She put up another two questions:

Is democracy dead? and *What can you do about the demagogues?*

A tall, brown haired student called Bryce took it up.

Bryce: "The story of democracy can be told as by a dad explaining it to his kids; 'we have a choice between ice cream, chocolate or sandwiches. Which of us gets to choose what we get if we can have only one?' 'Me', says the dad, 'because I'm the one with all the money'. A simple story and a lot rings true with it. Basically, the voting system isn't working nowadays, and the young are certainly disenfranchised."

Eleri responded to Bryce, nodding: "A good picture of the current democracy that we live in. The BMJ (British Medical Journal) brought out an article criticising many MPs, mainly Tories, who have been heavily involved with the Institute for Economic Affairs. This organisation is taking money off British American Tobacco and they are pushing for a form of populist free-marketism which decries the 'nanny state' to help keep us 'plebs' pumping smoke, alcohol and sugar into our bodies."

Bryce: "Regarding the demagogues, I guess getting the truth out to as many people as possible is a good thing, but as I mentioned around democracy, those with the money have the loudest voices, there has been an awful lot of fake news going around in recent years and I've been surprised by some of the people who have mistaken it for truth."

Eleri: "Narrative is often more important than facts for people. Political allegiances for instance may have ideas that are based more on beliefs than facts, but people buy into them, sometimes because of conformity, or emulating parents, that kind of thing.

In the 90s two psychologists managed to penetrate a cult in America, with a woman at its centre who claimed the world was going to end but that her group was going to get saved by aliens. The psychologists were intrigued as to what the cultists would do when the day she said the world would end came around.

The psychologists were surprised that when the date and time came and went the cultists made excuses and felt even more committed rather than duped. The leader of the cult just said the date had changed and made up another one. Many of the people who had joined had given up jobs and families so felt committed. Many times in life, people can delude themselves. This is just an extreme example."

Bryce: "Wow, that explains a fair bit from the last few years!"

Eleri: "Yes, for instance the 'low tax' narrative pushed by the right is clearly very flawed. Less tax simply means fewer services, apart from for the few who can afford them. It's their story though."

Wrapping things up, Eleri added: "Traditional strategies like voting, lobbying and protests have stopped working because of the deep interests of political and economic forces. We'll have a debate over these issues next week."

*

Bangor was a pretty place really, but this had become lost on Eleri. Her thoughts would often wander back to Jordan, her mother, the struggles of her friend Penny, and the culprits who had brought about a 'war on the poor'.

The politics she looked upon seemed ludicrous. People telling lies and creating division appeared the norm. Lies told by the affluent and paid for by the poor and doing nobody's mental health any good. The politicians who would say absolutely anything to gain or retain power and who would be caught on camera saying black is black one day, and adamant that black is, in actual fact, white the next. Nobody believed them. How did they sleep at night driving such hateful narratives that negatively impacted the lives of millions of people?

It was like the opposite of the stoic philosophy, *"if it is not right do not do it, if it is not true do not say it."*

Eleri looked at the big increase in the number of foodbanks, the rise and rhetoric of the far right, the slagging and diminishment of the NHS, the denial of climate change, the blaming of immigrants for society's woes. It fed her hatred and when some of the liars and charlatans came on TV, Eleri's face became white and an evil sneer ran across her face. It was like seeing and listening to pigs, corrupted, like in George Orwell's Animal Farm.

They lived isolated from most of society, and rarely, if ever, used the same services as normal people. Their parents weren't going to need the NHS and care homes, they'd pay for them privately and so were happy to fuck over the socialist endeavours first set forth by the likes of Nye Bevan and the efforts from that past generation.

She thought about the damage they'd done, the money wasted that could have gone towards education and health. They'd damaged millions of lives and some lives, such as her brother's and pretty much her mother's, had fucking ended.

*

On her monthly visit to her dad's to see how he was doing, she went back into her old room that she'd shared with Megan. She sat down on Megan's bed and looked at the wall opposite. It was still there, the picture of the Morrigan that Isabelle had given her when they were kids and the one next to it that Isabelle had given her when they were teens, commemorating setting off the gunpowder in one of the big slate holes.

She'd dedicated much of her life in trying to reduce inequality, and, staring at the image of the dark goddess with its lifelike eyes staring back, she reached a decision. It felt like a 'eureka' moment in her mind, a commitment. The powerful needed to pay for what they had wrought and she would bring some justice to them. The formal justice systems worldwide that people knew clearly worked for them, they were in their pocket just as Al Capone had Chicago's police in his, this was just on a wider scale. Journalists getting silenced for asking questions about millionaires and billionaires doing questionable things. There was no accountability for the liars. The feeling was powerful in her, it felt like her whole body and blood craved justice.

"**ENOUGH, ENOUGH, ENOUGH!**" she thought as she stood up angrily. But what could she do about it? What could anyone do to change it? Voting was a joke and the people at the top were effectively extremists protected by wealth and lies.

It would take something extraordinary to take on the type of people who had gained power. How does somebody take on the most powerful extremists? Do you have to become an extremist yourself, where the end justifies any means. Eleri's thoughts flowed wildly, thinking about every mad possibility.

*

After a month of sleeping exceedingly badly with mad ideas taking up much of her mental bandwidth, she dreamed of Jordan. His voice whispered to her from the grave. They were sat by the fire in her and Zoe's old house in Brynrefail, just the two of them, each with a cup of peppermint tea in hand, sharing a joint and well on the way to crumbling completely.

Jordan: "We were pretty rinsed after the music stopped and headed into the far end of the catacombs. Nobody really goes there because it's as far from the music or the entrance as you can get. There was a small hole in the wall near the ground, just enough to crawl through. I was with Marve. He was too big to get through. It was full of boxes Eleri, big metal boxes with padlocks on, I think there were a few barrels too. I wasn't hallucinating so don't laugh. We should go back there sometime, Eleri, with bolt cutters and see what's inside them."

Eleri: "It was used for storing munitions during World War Two, no way would they have left anything in there though. You want to watch what you're taking at these parties."

Jordan gave her a soft punch on the arm jokingly.

Eleri woke up sweating. Was that a dream, or was that one of her and Jordan's chats when tired at an after party? She thought back to the conversation she'd had with Zoe about the nitroglycerin exploding in Cwm Y Glo. Had she dreamed that conversation too? She had slept so badly the last month her memory wasn't working too well. It was just a dream, she was sure. But later in the week she started to wonder more and more about the catacombs and Jordan's words, "we should go back there sometime, Eleri."

Jordan wouldn't ever be going back to explore, but Eleri would be. Some days after the dream and after collecting some bolt cutters from B&Q, she drove to Llanberis and hiked down to the bunker where she'd once been to the odd rave. Memories flooded back to her; having a great time with friends, dancing, music, kissing Jacob and walking out into the dawn...Jordan and this dream she'd had.

She made a rollie whilst staring at the entrance and then lit it as she entered the catacombs. Headtorch in her hand, she made her way inwards and then up the stairs and started a thorough search of the far end, where revellers had generally avoided. After half an hour of scouting, Eleri began wondering if she truly had lost it, following the breadcrumbs of a dream, when suddenly she found the very small hole near one corner. It was damp and some sort of seepage had caused the concrete to corrode away, leaving the small hole.

She wondered how the fuck her brother had fit through it and was worried that he had been hallucinating, or that she was. After a couple of minutes of contemplating uncharitable thoughts about her dead brother and her memory she crawled through and shone her headtorch around.

Jordan hadn't been hallucinating. Eleri's memory wasn't totally screwed. The room was full of metal boxes. There was no writing on the boxes. Getting her bolt cutters out of the small rucksack, she set to on the first padlock and after much squeezing, and some cursing, the bastard eventually cut through.

Lifting the lid carefully, Eleri peered her torch inside and a smile bloomed on her face, the light of her torch reflecting off her glasses.

CHAPTER 12: Y BRENHINOEDD MOCH (THE PIG KINGS)

It was hard to tell if it was real or not. What was going on? Was everyone everywhere on acid? Perhaps it was only a dream.

*

Across the island of Britain it appeared to even people of sound mind that a story such as one found in books, such as the Mabinogion or Animal Farm, had indeed come to pass. For many millions it appeared that a powerful magician had used magic on the leaders of the island so that the leader thought themselves very smart and righteous, whereas for anyone with common sense it was clear to see that these leaders and their close ilk were the most horrible of pigs. Neither smart nor moral, they'd built their kingdom on lies, deceit, and division, and all the pig kings and their closest hogs would happily tell the people in Britain that day was night and night was day, without blushing, without any shame.

Most of the pig kings had come from the same sty where they were brought up and taught all they knew. They were taught that they were better than everyone else, that bullying was encouraged and a sense of absolute entitlement and ambition for power was engraved into their little pig souls. Sadly, they were never taught right from wrong or to fear shame, they were pushed only towards the quest for fame.

Two smug pigs who were particularly keen on pushing austerity chatted with each other in an ivory tower:

Smug pig 1: "Oink, oink, oink", which meant; *'I'm glad we fucked over the poor and got away with saying we were just being fiscally responsible. The NHS will have to be privatised in the not-too-distant future, thanks to our decisions. None of the statisticians or other boffs are bright enough to work out how little we've spent on health in comparison with other countries.'*

Smug pig 2: "Oink, oink, oink", which meant; *'We used to chat about these plans in our sty schoolyard, remember? I wish I was still the king of the pigs, I enjoyed ruling and running things down for the poor plebs. By increasing the inequality and making most people poorer it will make it easier for our children to become leaders, because they'll be some of the few who have had a decent education and can afford healthcare.'*

The two pigs smiled at each other smugly, both believing themselves very smart indeed.

*

The truth rarely came out of the new pig king's mouth. Known to all as BJ, he had stirred hatred of foreigners amongst the Britons to make them angry. He publicised his racist remarks, had a good go at gay people, dissed single mothers, embraced racist nutcases from across the ocean and took on board their ideas. The pig had pushed for Brexit which flushed tens of billions of pounds down the shithole that could have been put into health and education. It also wasted a great deal of people's time on ludicrous arguments. He'd hid from any interviews to avoid scrutiny before the little boars voted him as their leader. This was a most cowardly pig king. That he looked like a total mess in appearance and lacked any coherence in his speeches was the least of this king's foibles.

To help him become the pig king he'd had the help of a very clever hog, called Dim. Dim was such a smart pig, and although he was not from the same sty he had a similar ethos, that the end justifies any means.

Between BJ and Dim they enjoyed creating a very hateful political message. Some politicians questioned them on the horrible politics they'd created and were actually worried for their lives. But they just answered as you'd expect true pigs to.

Pig king: "Oink, Oink," which meant; *'bar humbug!'*

"Oink, Oink, Oink," which meant; *'get bullshit done then.'*

These little piggies didn't care about death threats and people's lives at all.

"Oink, oink, oink," laughed BJ now that he'd taken in all the poor Britons and told them he'd be levelling them all up. BJ would say anything and didn't mind if it was the opposite of the truth. The levelling up line really was a total lie after all. In truth, he just wanted to sell off the NHS - it was socialist after all, and him and his team of pigs hated socialism and anything connected to it. Once it was gone, the poor would be even poorer as they'd have to try and pay for health care.

"Oink, oink, oink," thought BJ, reflecting on how the streets of Britain would be like America's cities and full of poor homeless fuckers who couldn't afford health insurance.

"Oink, oink, oink." The king of the pigs snorted a line of coke. It was 11am and the pig king would have to get up and start some work soon. He tried to do as little work as possible normally. He was meant to be at an emergency meeting of some kind, but instead he put on the TV and watched one of his favourite cartoons from his childhood, the Hair Bear Bunch.

His pig party were having a crackdown on people using drugs, but this crackdown was for normal people, not for the pigs within his party, who needed a great deal of drugs to get through each day. It definitely helps to be high as fuck when you are forced to tell so many porky tales for the pig king and then deny what has been caught on camera. The pig king's closest allies were all high as fuck most of the time, which is how most of them managed to get to sleep at night after living such deeply shameful lives during the daytime.

BJ: "Oink, oink," which meant 'Hi', to Judas, his head of security, as he opened the door. Judas didn't seem too smart to BJ, but it made him feel safe having him around. He had a hell of a CV. However, his very cold blue eyes did look like they were waiting to carve somebody up. BJ vaguely recalled someone saying that he may well have done just that, something of a Jason Bourne-like character. Judas nodded back and they made their way downstairs.

The king of pigs gathered the smaller pigs around.

"Oink, oink, oink," he said, meaning he was worried about the report which had been written about Russian interference in the referendum.

"Oink," said the clever pig, Dim, which meant, 'just sit on it and don't let the public read it'.

"Oink, oink, oink," laughed the king pig.

"Oink, oink, oink," he continued, which meant he didn't like what one of the TV channels had been saying about him or his little pigs.

"Oink," said Dim, which meant they'd try to privatise the channel or try to get some of their little pigs to be put in charge of it.

"Oink, oink, oink," laughed the king of the pigs smugly, and the other smaller pigs also laughed. It was all so funny, they could say and do anything they wanted to, however mean and untrue. Like magic from ancient stories, many people believed them or were too apathetic to do anything about it.

The pigs kept reducing the services and opportunities for most people but told them these were the best services and opportunities they had ever had... as the foodbank queues got longer.

"Oink, oink oink," lied the pigs, all the time, every day. Lying was what the pig kings did best. Ambition had taken them to some dark places indeed.

An unkindness of ravens flew towards all the pigs and shat on their heads.

*

A dream, no, a nightmare for sure. Fucking psychedelics.

CHAPTER 13:
YMARFER (PRACTICE)

It was quite a stockpile! It took Eleri several weeks between her lecturing work to get a lot of it out of the bunker and make a pile of the munitions in her spare room on Goodman street. In fact, it was too large even for the spare room; she had some of it in the loft, some in cupboards, under her bed and also in boxes that she sealed up with gaffer tape in the utility room. She'd read up about some of the items she had collected and realised that the redness of the water in the catacombs was due to the TNT in the barrels. Thinking back, she wondered how that poor party-goer got on after falling in...

There were several large barrels in the room where it was clearly once used to store various anti-tank weapons. There was even a box full of Blacker Bombards; some units during WW2 had refused to use them, which could have explained why some had been left forgotten about in the catacombs. There seemed to be an awful lot of Mills bomb, Thermos and Hawkins grenades. There were also a couple of boxes of M102 shells which were the heaviest to carry, weighing in at a bit over 40 kilos each.

She hoped beyond hope that there wasn't an accident which took out the whole street but she'd gotten into the mindset that risks had to be taken and collateral damage was inevitable. She told no one what she was up to and became a creature of the night for a while between her lectures. Her friends tried to get her out for a drink, a climb or a party but she was absorbed in her new crusade. When Osian, Zoe and Lewis messaged her to get out she fobbed them off saying she was too busy with work at the moment.

She wanted to see if the gear she'd found still worked, after all it was meant for battles in WW2 and had been sat for decades. She knew the ideal spot for testing, in the base of some of the huge slate holes in the quarries she'd explored plenty as a child.

She started with a small test at first. She went into the quarries around twilight and in her waistcoat pocket she carried just three Mills bomb grenades, shaped like small metal pineapples.

Standing at the top of Twll Mawr as the sun went down, she made sure there was nobody coming from either direction on the public right of way. The Llanberis Pass could be made out, a huge gap between the sides of Glyder Fawr and Crib Goch, the view she'd loved to see with her family growing up and when climbing with her friends in the quarries.

As the darkness settled she looked into the huge pit and, taking one of the grenades out, she pulled the pin and threw it out as far as she could into the night, over and into the big slate hole.

The seconds stretched like eternity for Eleri but she had researched how long in theory it should take for detonation and as she heard a light clang with the grenade hitting the ground there was suddenly a burst of light and sound which threw Eleri's shadow against the back wall of slate some way behind her.

BOOM

She took the pins out of the other two grenades and lobbed them in too, to make sure of the efficacy. She thought any researcher worth their money would have done the same.

The seconds didn't seem as long this time and, as with the first test, when the grenades hit the base of the hole more than

200 feet below, they released their awful power. The noise could certainly have been heard from Llanberis and Eleri hoped they just took it for a rock fall. She'd timed the period from pulling the pin to detonation for each, around four seconds in total. She'd read up about these things and apparently the British Home Guard had been told they could be thrown 30 yards, but had a danger area of 100 yards!

As she turned to head back to her car she stopped and looked over her shoulder, sensing that she was being watched. However, peering around into the dark shadows, there were no sounds and she could see nothing there.

As she left the hole, down the path towards her car a bespectacled man watched her leaving, hidden high up above the hole. He'd been watching the detonations and he was wondering what the fuck she was up to.

*

Next time Eleri went into the quarries she tackled the same ladders she had taken many years before with Zoe and Isabelle to access the base of the huge holes of Mordor and through the connecting tunnel to the Lost World. On the walk, Eleri admired the Mackerel sky, its presence indicating that a weather front could be on the way in. Her dad had been the first to tell her of different types of clouds but her favourite teacher, Miss Smith, had helped drill it in when studying weather systems in Geography.

When she arrived in the base of the huge Lost World hole, she looked around with her headtorch. The little house made of slate was still there and so was the rock she'd set the small explosion off.

She went inside and after a rummage about under some moss she rediscovered the powdwr du. She carried most of the bags back through the tunnel and deposited them there, intending to increase her stockpile in her spare room. She didn't think it would be worth much on top of the stuff she already had. She'd brought down a few bucketloads of TNT on separate visits and had put this in a plastic box in the centre of the building. There was no way she was carrying one of the M102 shells down, the weight of one of them might have caused her to have an accident getting down the old ladders. The TNT at least seemed easy to manoeuvre around and considerably less prone to accidents than nitroglycerin from what she'd read.

Hanging from a tunnel high in the rockface 100 feet to her right was an old 9mm climbing rope she'd left there. She put her extra munitions into the small slate house and taped a grenade securely to a large piece of heavy slate forming part of the door of the house. She then connected the old rope to the pin of the grenade via a knot and a metal karabiner. She climbed the first ladders which led upwards and gained the tunnel mouth where she had left the old rope hanging down. Looking down on the house over 100 feet below in the twilight, she gave another inspection of the hole she was in to make sure there were no people or animals who might get hit by the shrapnel. Seeing it was clear she took hold of the rope with both hands and, moving so she was sheltered from the blast, she pulled hard on the rope.

BOOM

The slate walls shook and the earth grumbled. Slate shards shot past the mouth of Eleri's tunnel and a few huge pieces of rock came apart from above the tunnel mouth somewhere and hurtled down, giving Eleri only a vague feeling of intense danger as they went past.

"Fuck," Eleri whispered, crouching down with hands covering both of her ears, the blast considerably louder than she'd expected. After a minute of crouching she returned to the mouth of the tunnel and looked down, still cursing and holding her forearm which had gained a deep cut from a small piece of slate that had managed to ricochet into her tunnel.

Through the slate dust and smoke from the blast she could see just clearly enough that the small slate house no longer existed. She'd used only the smallest amount of what was in her spare room. Very satisfactory. With the sort of fire power she had, there were a multitude of possible plans she could make. The pain in her forearm evaporated as her mind started working.

On the opposite side of the hole, the same bespectacled head that had been snooping on Eleri a few days earlier finally braved to raise his head and inspect the blast zone, fingers still nursing his sore ears. He could make out her headtorch in the tunnel mouth, before she turned and disappeared from view. He was now extremely concerned about what was going on but was unsure what to do about it.

"Fucking fuck," he whispered into the night.

Eleri climbed out of the last set of ladders and hiked through the quarries down to her home in Llanberis, her mind playing with options.

When she got in she made a brew, set the fire and began chain smoking rollies while watching the fire, and scribbling on A3 paper. A bus, gear from spare room, generator, speakers, ropes, reinforced steel segments, ravens, the picture of the Morrigan from her and Megan's old childhood room, Jordan's slate engraving from his grave. The list went on. It would certainly take some time to prepare.

Finding a day when most of the culprits were together wouldn't be easy, but Eleri kept her eye on the news. She was also very much a pragmatist. Most of them would have to do, some rats would always get away.

After several months of trawling through the bullshit news

they threw out she found it, eyebrows raised high above her glasses. She looked at who was going to be there, the lying smirker, the austerity pushers, the immigrant-bashing racist and his sidekick, loads of rich money laundering schizers who had pushed austerity on the poor. What was the date going to be? 31st October. Halloween. This would be appropriate indeed. A true festival of bullshit that she could gatecrash. It was set to be in an area of Hyde Park, not a part of London Eleri knew well, but one which was easy to research.

A knock at the door brought her out of her euphoria at finally having a date, and only a bit over a month away at that.

Penny: "Eleri, it's me!"

"Shit," Eleri mouthed. She'd totally forgotten Penny was coming over this weekend. Grabbing her scribbled plans, she chucked them into the spare room and locked the door. She'd gotten into the habit of locking it over the last few months, since using it for munitions storage.

Eleri: "Hi Penny! Sorry I got embroiled in my work then, didn't hear the door."

Penny: "No problem, give me a hand in. Thomas gave me a lift on the bus, he can talk can't he! And still hasn't kicked the fags."

Eleri helped Penny over the step and into the living room and got her a glass of red wine to have by the fire. The flames were keeping the chill of autumn at bay and throwing out an orange glow along with the odd bit of wood smoke.

Eleri: "None of us have managed to kick the fags but yeah, he can talk for Wales. How have you been?"

Penny: "Not too great recently to be honest, you know they've reduced the Personal Independence Payment, and my employment and support allowance I get. You know, I've been using a foodbank for a while now, I hear even some nurses need to use some now, and they earn a lot more than I do. It makes me feel a bit shamed, like they have taken some chips out of my dignity with a pick axe."

Eleri: "Oh Penny, that's shit."

The conversation continued in a similar vein, chatting about Penny's hardships and those of her close friends in Birmingham. After a while, and after months of keeping her plan strictly to herself, Eleri started to fish with Penny.

Eleri: "What do you think of the people who have made these decisions which have caused you and your friends such hardship Penny?"

Penny: "What do you think I think of them Eleri? The same as you, I detest them. I've seen it in your eyes too."

Eleri could see that Penny was thinking on the same wavelength as her, but changed the subject onto more mellow and mundane themes and heated them up some of the curry she'd made the night before. As the spare room was full of munitions Eleri set up the sofa bed in the living room for Penny, apologising for her 'work equipment' filling the spare.

The next morning Eleri had one lecture to give and said sorry to Penny for disappearing for a few hours. She was gobsmacked that she had forgotten Penny was coming to visit, but her focus had narrowed the last few months so there was little conscious bandwidth for other things.

While Eleri was out, Penny made herself coffee and tea and noticed that the spare room had a lock on it, which naturally made her curious. Eleri had never been one to keep secrets and Penny was sure she wouldn't mind her having a snoop. Penny wheeled around the living room a bit, hunting for a key. After a few minutes of searching she was about to give up and just ask Eleri for a peek when she was back, but looking up at the kettle she saw a key hanging from a piece of string. She grabbed it and tried it in the door lock. She pushed the door open and her eyes widened in surprise. She spent the next hour doing internet searches to work out exactly what was in the spare room, then locked it up again and waited for Eleri's return.

A few hours later Eleri bustled through the door.

Penny: "Want a coffee? I'll stick one on."

Eleri: "Ace, thanks Penny."

Penny's eyes kept glancing towards the spare room.

Sipping her coffee, Eleri asked where Penny would like to go in the afternoon but noticed where Penny's eyes kept swerving to and looked to the key by the kettle.

She stared at Penny, nodding to herself.

Eleri: "Have you taken a look inside then?"

Penny went red in the face.

Penny: "Sorry Eleri, I couldn't resist. When I was making brews I clocked the key and just had a little look. It's quite the stockpile you've got there, I hope you're not into arms dealing for Saudi Arabia or anything nefarious like that."

Eleri had been thinking about Penny overnight. She'd kept her plans all to herself so far, but she trusted Penny more than she trusted anyone.

Eleri: "What would you be willing to give, Penny, if you were given the opportunity to send the people making these decisions a clear message, the people at the very top, who have been responsible for so much misery. What about a chance to question the key culprits?"

Penny: "What have you got in mind Eleri? I swear I won't tell anyone, whatever it involves."

Eleri: "To be part of it we'll quite literally need to be 'all in'. The plan I've come up with is most probably a one-way trip."

Penny nodded and, looking determined, smiled.

Penny: "I still want to be part of it Eleri, I meant what I said."

Eleri chatted through what she'd been up to the last few months, the message from Jordan, the catacombs, the successful tests she'd run in the quarry holes, the festival of bullshit.

Penny: "Jesus, good effort Eleri. What's the date we are going down?"

Eleri: "Halloween."

Penny smiled again: "Very good. I've never liked November, not since my mother passed away."

Penny hung out for a few days and then Eleri ran her back to Birmingham. They picked up things she needed for the lead up to Halloween, as from then on Penny would be helping in Llanberis with the preparations. Penny's time as a librarian had not been idle and she was assiduous with task and finish lists and came up with a few points and possible scenarios they might contend with that made Eleri very grateful for her being there.

Penny left a note for Jane and Dan, her work colleagues at the library, to apologise and say she was struggling a bit and had gone to stay with a relative for the foreseeable. She also texted her friend Barbara who she'd met at the foodbank to tell her not to worry. There wasn't a lot she'd miss about her current life in Birmingham, which had felt like it was being diminished more and more year by year. The opportunity Eleri was providing to meet the culprits seemed like a golden ticket indeed.

Although mainly busy with Penny and planning, Eleri did take a night off from the tasks and met up with Isabelle who she'd not seen in months. They met up in the Glyntwrog pub and on their second pint what Isabelle had to tell her sent a chill down her spine, even though it was clearly of little significance to Isabelle.

Isabelle: "Yeah, the cops came to the house and asked if I knew of anyone letting off explosives in the quarry. I jokingly mentioned you doing that as a kid. Do you remember when you burned your eyebrows?"

Isabelle now lived in Dinorwic, not far from the main quarries.

Eleri: "What did they say to that?"

She nervously wondered if they'd be calling in at her house, which was brimming with explosives.

Isabelle: "Nothing eh, they weren't interested in what we were up to 20 years ago. It was probs just some kids letting off fireworks."

Eleri: "Funny. I did hear something loud one night a few weeks back."

Isabelle: "Me too, woke me up actually. Must have been some fucking firework."

Eleri: "You can buy big ones nowadays. I've got Penny staying with me at the moment. She's loving spending a bit of time here."

Isabelle: "Ace, gotta beat Birmingham hasn't it? She should move to this area, she's got plenty of friends here. I've got the cards you asked for."

Isabelle pulled out a small package from her colourful large handbag and handed it to Eleri. It was a packet of a hundred cards, each with a pencil drawing of eyes with raven's wings as the eyebrows.

Eleri: "These are perfect, thanks Isabelle."

These were going to be for the corrupt editors, journos and key shitheads at some of the 'thinktanks' who were in the hands of immoral billionaires trying to fuck over everyone in the world. It was a shame none of them would be at the festival.

CHAPTER 14: PARATOI (PREPARATION)

The largest and most critical piece of equipment Eleri and Penny needed was owned by an old friend of the family. Thomas, who used to drive her around on the buses, had become the manager of the depot, and many buses were often parked up on the outskirts of Deiniolen. He still drove occasionally if someone was sick, hence Penny fortuitously catching a ride with him.

Eleri went for a chat with him at the depot one afternoon, partly to see how he was doing and also to enquire about the older buses that were sat there. If her venture was successful, she wouldn't have to try and squeeze all the necessary equipment into a hired minibus.

Sitting on a bench together inside the complex next to six retired red buses, Eleri marvelled at how heavily Thomas could smoke and still be alive. By the time she rolled one fag, he'd smoked one and had rolled another, which went straight into his mouth.

Eleri: "Any romance at the mo, Thomas?"

Thomas grunted: "Usual stuff. I've started to use Tinder a bit, but feel a bit of a luddite with it. People's profiles are often nothing like the person you meet; not sure mine gives a great picture of me either."

Eleri: "It's a tough game out there nowadays."

Thomas: "It's always been the toughest game Eleri. I'm definitely feeling a bit old for it nowadays, might have to settle down at some point. I've not seen you at your folks' house recently, I know they'd both like to see you."

Eleri: "I'll pop in soon. Sorry I've been slack, it's been a mad few months with work. Do any of these buses still work Thomas?"

Thomas: "Of course, they just aren't quite reliable enough to be in service regularly anymore, most of them have a lot of mileage on their clocks. I still take a couple out for myself now and then, for old times' sake."

Eleri: "Could I buy one off you, off the depot? I'm thinking about renovating something like one of these to live in for a while. Some friends have land in Devon with a communal living area."

Thomas: "You ever driven a bus? Guess you've seen me driving them enough times. I could give you some lessons. You can have that one for free. It's the number 85 you came on with me for years, that took you to school and work in Bangor."

He pointed to one numbered 316 at the base.

Eleri: "For free? Are you sure? I don't want to take the piss, but I can guarantee it will be going to good use."

Thomas: "You are like a daughter to me Eleri. Ray is my best mate and I haven't any family anymore. I'd like to give you something; I might not be around too much longer either."

Eleri thought her heart had become glass over the last few years, but she felt a warmth at Thomas' words and she gave the small bear-like man a hug.

Eleri: "You'll be around forever Thomas. You are like one of the oak trees in the fields here."

Thomas: "The doc gave me some ambiguous news the other day Eleri. I've got a tumour on one of my lungs and they are trying to work out what to do about it. You should stop smoking you know, you are still young and you don't smoke much. I'd need a nicotine patch that covers my whole body to quit."

Eleri gave him another hug to hide the pain in her eyes.

Eleri: "You'll be alright, you'll probably smoke the tumour out with how much you still smoke!"

Thomas got up and limped over to the bus he was giving Eleri. His leg had gotten considerably worse over recent years. He threw Eleri a key.

Thomas: "You've been in this thing enough times, do you want to take me for a ride for a change?"

Eleri slid into the driver's seat and adjusted it to fit her. The cab smelled heavily of smoke, having had Thomas sat puffing in it for years.

Putting the key into the ignition, she twisted it and the bus started immediately, sounding pretty loud.

Thomas: "Key thing to remember is for any turn you make to give yourself plenty of room, go in an arc so that the side or back end isn't going to hit anything. Keep the revs high for starting in first or second gear too."

Eleri took it out of the depot, Thomas grinning beside her.

Eleri: "Where shall we go?"

Thomas: "Let's do a circular. Up the Llanberis Pass, around to Ogwen Valley and back to here. If you can drive that, you'll be ok on most roads."

They arrived in Llanberis after 10 minutes and a couple of Eleri's friends saw and waved in surprise at seeing her in a bus. Once over Pen y Pass and on the straighter roads towards Ogwen , Thomas grinned sensing Eleri's ability to handle the bus.

Thomas: "Open her up, let's see how fast she can go!"

Eleri put her foot down and Thomas took some heavy drags off his fag. They got towards 80 mph before slowing for the corners.

Thomas: "Not bad eh! Still got some life left in her, probably more than is left in me."

Eleri: "It's a million times better than driving my old car, that bloody escort."

As they sailed back down the Ogwen Valley Thomas leaned out of the window.

Thomas: "Always loved this view of Tryfan, it might be my favourite mountain. Ginger Cain has done a great painting of it, which is up in his shop, Llanberis Mountain Art."

Eleri smiled, thinking back to learning the ropes on some of the climbs up there with Lewis.

They made their way down to and through Bethesda, then headed back around to the depot at Deiniolen. Thomas stumbled out once they were parked up.

Thomas nodded to himself: "You can drive that as well as I can. Take it now if you like."

Eleri jumped down out of the bus, feeling elated from the drive and the time with Thomas. She gave him another hug.

Eleri: "Thanks so much Thomas, I'll try and look after her."

Thomas: "It's good to see it going to a good home to be honest."

Eleri waved goodbye to Thomas and drove her new vehicle back down to Llanberis, parking it next to Llyn Padarn at the lagoons, an array of tree-covered free car parks where all the van dossers stayed. She locked it up and stared at it in the fading light for a few minutes before making her way back to her house, thinking about renovations she'd need to do and people she'd need to get involved.

*

With only a month left to prepare, Eleri wasted no time and got various friends to help. One of the first things she did was get Isabelle and Maisy to paint huge ravens on each side of the bus and a woman's face on the front, with the tips of the ravens wings seeming to form the shoulders of the woman. It only took them half a day and resembled the image of the Morrigan that Eleri had in her mind.

Isabelle and Maisy grinned at Eleri and Penny when they'd finished.

Isabelle: "What do you think?"

Eleri: "It's beautiful you two! A banshee with a face of wrath; it's exactly what I wanted."

Penny: "You've got some skills there!"

Maisy: "I hope it doesn't scare the kids in this place in Devon you are moving to. It's not long until you're off there too."

Eleri: "Not long indeed. We'll be gone before Halloween."

She got Ug, Nodder, Jon and Lewis to strip a load of the chairs out from the back of the bus and take them to the dump. Eleri told them that she needed that extra space to put a bed in. The whole bus seemed full of green smoke by the time they'd ripped the chairs out and Eleri had to wait some time before going back in.

She needed the help of Osian and he duly arrived one afternoon in his green transporter with a load of metal sheets taking up much of the room inside the van. He jumped out and gave Eleri a hug, still sporting his blonde curly hair, super thick glasses and bulky forearms.

Osian: "I've got what you were after Eleri. Let's take a look at your new home then. You want a metal steel plate which can drop to cover the windscreen form the inside and some for the side windows? Have you been watching Mad Max?"

Eleri blushed. This particular part of the plan she had got from the first Mad Max, a film about a dystopian future where people are fighting over the last reserves of oil, in which they had vehicles that had been adapted for battles.

Eleri: "I might end up parking it in some pretty gnarly areas for some of my work. I don't want unwanted dickheads getting inside."

Osian nodded his head sceptically as he inspected the front of the bus.

Before long, he'd taken some measurements and set to welding some hinges into the roof of the bus. Eleri smoked and watched the sparks fly out of the door of the bus as Osian worked his magic.

Between the two of them, they managed to attach the front windscreen barrier to the roof, with a rope through a pulley on the floor of the bus allowing it to be lowered into place with ease, thankfully for Eleri, and locked into place at its base. It had a small lookout hole in the plate so she could still see out of the barrier somewhat.

Eleri had been impressed with Osian's work over the years, and the speed with which he upgraded the front of the bus in just a matter of hours really was something to behold. Smaller metal side panels went up on the front interior of the van and across the door, which could be flicked up and across the door and locked into place quickly, and, combined with the front barrier, would form a very sturdy-looking bus front.

Osian: "That should stop most chavs getting in the front. It will take me some time to make you a metal mask like the bad guy from Mad Max Two mind."

Eleri punched him, then gave him a hug.

Eleri: "Thanks a lot pal, it's exactly what I was after. It means I'll be able to get some sleep without worrying. Penny might well be joining me in it too".

Where some of the chairs had been ripped out, Eleri put a mattress, as her and Penny would be spending a night on the road. She built several large cupboards from 2x4s and plywood, which would be storage areas used for the munitions at some point. The thought of getting it all into these areas gave her a headache, but at least it would be a much lesser task than getting it out of the bunker.

It still took Eleri several days to get all the munitions into the cupboards, and her back ached after finishing the job. The explosives weighed a good deal and the bus looked to sit a bit lower than before. She pursed her lips wondering if it would affect the bus's speed much, but figured there wasn't much she could do about that.

*

Eleri was alone a couple of evenings later, inspecting the bus interior when it was pretty much finished. She'd slotted the generator into place, moved the big speakers they'd used for the odd rave in the front and she'd even got two amps, remembering Jordan's tip off just in case one didn't work. She was content with the set up.

Going to the door, the daylight was fading fast as dusk descended. She was surprised by the face that was coming towards her. There was no forgetting that face and she was truly shocked when he started to speak, she'd heard that he couldn't, or wouldn't.

Smiler: "You know your brother died because he was depressed Eleri. It wasn't anyone's fault, not yours, not your mum's. I could see it in him, darkness."

Eleri was dumbstruck at hearing him speak at first, but slowly digested his words before responding.

Eleri: "Thank you. I knew he could get depressed, but from what I've pieced together it looks like he went to bits when he lost his job."

Smiler: "Like I said, it's just one of them things. People lose jobs all the time, it was more than that with Jordan."

Eleri: "Well. Losing his job was a big factor in his death and in my mother no longer speaking. And I think some people are to blame for my brother and many others losing their jobs, becoming impoverished, suffering and, in the case of my brother, paying the ultimate price."

Smiler: "You know he'd had an affair too? It can play on someone's mind that kind of thing."

Eleri wondered how the fuck he knew about that and started to feel a bit creeped out.

Eleri: "You seem to have been keeping an eye on me and my brother! I'm sorry about your loss, mine feels like a black hole inside of me too."

It didn't seem possible, but Eleri was sure Smiler's face became even more pained, which seemed impossible, and she regretted trying to empathise with the feeling of loss. It must have been two decades ago or more he lost his child, but the memories clearly still cutdeep.

Smiler: "I've seen you in the quarries, experimenting with danger. I've heard that you do some good work around equality stuff. It would be a shame to lose you."

With that, Smiler turned around and walked off, face still painted in pain.

Eleri stared after him wondering how much he knew. If he'd have stuck around, she'd have educated him that it was *equity* she worked in and that *equality* was often bullshit, giving freebies to people who didn't need them. Smiler had clearly been watching her and Jordan for some time, even though it appeared he had no interest in anything in life. She remembered he attended Jordan's funeral, so clearly he did care about some things.

*

Eleri went for a chat with Megan one evening a few days before her and Penny were due to depart. Megan and Cai had lasted the distance since school and had lived in Caernarfon for a number of years, in a three-bedroom semi-detached house within sight of the Morrisons.

Eleri had seen little of her sister for the last few months, between her work and preparation they never seemed to cross paths at their parent's house. Eleri found it pretty hard seeing Megan and Gwawr together, as it always evoked memories of Jordan.

Megan and Cai were thinking about having kids soon and it brought into Eleri's mind the sharp contrast between the different trajectories they were planning to take.

Megan gave her a wide smile and a hug when she answered the door, before making her a panad. Cai was at work.

Megan: "How have you been?"

Eleri: "Not bad. Sorry I've not been round for a bit, had a lot on at work."

Megan: "You look well anyway. Cai tells me you've got one of Thomas' buses he used to take us on, a fine sentimental piece I hope?"

Eleri blushed: "It was kind of him to give me it, it still drives well. I'll be taking it down south in a few days. I may not be back for a while."

Megan: "You got a fella down there? I thought you were settled here again. Get him to move up!"

Eleri: "No guy involved in this. You might call it business I guess, bit of a project which is culminating. Sorry I won't be around to help with mum and dad."

Megan: "Don't worry about it. I'm there twice a week. Thomas does the same and Ray likes a bit of down time with her. He's changed quite a bit too over the last few years. I wish he'd stop smoking though, same with you, you're too old for it now."

Eleri relaxed a bit at Megan's kind words.

Eleri: "You and Cai have done well here, it's a lovely home."

Megan: "Thanks, we'll get you round more often when you are back. You could be an auntie soon, hopefully."

Eleri: "You'll be a great mum, and Cai a great dad. You might even get mum talking again."

Megan: "I hope so, dad will love it at least."

Eleri handed Megan a large, packed envelope.

Eleri: "This is for your birthday, as I'll miss it. Promise me not to open it until then."

Megan: "Thank you Eleri, you're always too generous though. Are you going to stay for dinner? Cai will be back soon."

Eleri shook her head.

Eleri: "I'd better get back, Penny's been staying and is cooking something up. Please say hi to Cai though. Tell him to quit the tabs too, not a good habit for a dad."

Eleri gave Megan a hug much like the one Jordan had given her before he disappeared.

"You've got to quit too!" Megan shouted after Eleri as she made her way over to her Almera.

She didn't have the heart to visit Gwawr and Ray so near to her departure, and her chat with Megan had shown the two sisters going in very different directions. She was chuffed for Megan.

When Eleri got back Penny had a pasta pesto feast ready and the fire was roaring. Lighting up a rollie after the meal and sharing a glass of red wine, Eleri whispered just three words to Penny.

"We are ready."

CHAPTER 15: Y TAITH (THE JOURNEY)

The 30th of October arrived and, after a relaxed morning and a hearty lunch of sweet potato, butternut squash and ginger soup, Eleri and Penny made their way down to the lagoons. The weather was bleak, with persistent light rain and a fairly strong breeze. The rain and wind made it tricky for Eleri to see through her glasses and she kicked herself for not trying out contact lenses. Squinting as they neared the bus, she could begin to make out a small blue panda parked nearby. As they got nearer, Lewis hopped out with a big round dish covered in foil in one hand. The rain started to form a sheen on his long, wavy hair and the breeze made him look ripe for a shampoo advert, thought Eleri, although his face was probably a bit too pasty from the lack of sun in the area.

Lewis: "Iawn guys, I came to see you both off. You'll be missed. Bryony made you this quiche for the drive. Osian and Zoe were sorry they couldn't see you off, they're both at work today."

Eleri and Penny gave Lewis a hug and thanked him for bringing the food.

Penny: "Thank Bryony for the quiche Lewis, it smells lovely. We'll look forward to this later!"

Eleri set the ramp up on the doorstep and helped Penny up into the bus.

Lewis: "When do you think you'll be back?"

Eleri: "Early next year hopefully. The main thing is to finish the project we've been working on."

Lewis: "I hope it goes well! The bus is looking mean anyway."

Eleri chucked Lewis the keys for her Almera.

Eleri: "Can you give those to Isabelle? Tell her it's hers, certainly for the winter. My house keys are on there and the DVLA documents are on my living room table."

Lewis: "No worries, I'll let her know Eleri."

Eleri stuck on the first track of a playlist she'd made; Lost in Music by Sister Sledge. She smiled and waved at Lewis as she closed the door and got the bus started, engine purring as they left the lagoons. She'd gone back to the cemetery and picked up the heavy slate plaque from her brother's grave and had it sat beside her. As they made their way through Llanberis, they saw a van burning in the council estate on the right as they went past the Victoria Hotel. Eleri took it as a positive omen and one certainly apt for all the chaotic politics those fools had brought into play.

Making their way up the Llanberis Pass, Eleri looked to Penny.

Eleri: "Are you happy Penny?"

Penny smiled: "As happy as I've ever been. I've fond memories of this journey. The first time I came here was with you on the way from Birmingham. It feels like a lifetime ago, but it has only been a few years."

The waterfalls were in spate between the cliff faces on either side of the road on the way up the Llanberis Pass. Autumnal leaves in various shades of gold and brown were blowing around, sometimes in small whirlwinds. A few of the cliffs held fond memories for Eleri and, remembering how she took Jordan up some of the easier climbs to show him the ropes, she wondered what he would have thought about her and Penny's course of action.

He'd often seemed a little bit 'tapped' in a quiet, mercurial and dark kind of way and his disappearance from Eleri's world had ignited something quite spectacular in her, something which demanded going right to the edge and beyond, a wave which had built up over several years and which would soon be released. It would certainly be doing the world a favour. The police clearly weren't going to lock these people up, which would have been the ideal solution.

She ruminated a little about why she could not just suck it up like most people would and, like Smiler had recommended, treat it as a normal tragedy for someone who got a bit depressed and get on with her life. It was a momentary thought that was quickly tamped down by the statistics that she knew so well, a number her brother had become part of. The disgusting creatures who had somehow grabbed the reins of power needed karma brought their way, and she intended to do just that.

They summited over Pen-y-Pass and slowly descended down and along towards Capel Curig as Metallica's Nothing Else Matters came on. As they neared the wooded town of Betws-y-Coed, the rain stopped and a few miles further down the A5 the clouds parted and some rays of sun shone through. Age of Consent by Bronski Beat came on, and then Radiohead's Planet Telex, before Eleri put on Decomposed Radio 047, a reminder of her and Penny's first journey along the A5.

They both put their shades on as the windscreen wipers stopped and the sun made it hard to see without them, nodding to the music and enjoying the scenery.

Penny started to read after a time.

Eleri: "What's the book?"

Penny: "Eon, a book by Greg Bear I told you about. It's what the films 2001 and Interstellar are loosely based around, with the cold war going on, a huge oblong asteroid arrives above the earth and the Americans and Soviets start fighting over it.

Nuclear war breaks out as a few people are stuck watching in the chambers of the rock. The seventh chamber inside seems to go on forever, a singularity. I've read it before but it's a great one to skim again, one of my favourites."

Eleri: "I remember you telling me about it. Doesn't seem that unfeasible a storyline going off the last few years."

They left the rolling hills behind them and went around Shrewsbury near the end of the A5, Penny still engrossed in her book. As they meandered onto the M6 through Birmingham, Eleri wondered if Penny felt any longing for home, or regret for joining her on a truly mad venture.

These were the last few hours where they could make a U-turn if they wished and nobody would be any the wiser. They could let the liars and charlatans make things worse for millions of people and get on with their lives, turning a blind eye to it, pretending that their vote had an impact. Eleri had a lot of experience of dealing with anxiety before setting off on climbs which would test her, and she had similar feelings as the miles ticked by. A bit past Birmingham the sun set and on the M40, they pulled into some services to refuel and use the toilets. They bought a couple of flat whites and big milkshakes before setting off back to the bus, Penny carrying the drinks and Eleri pushing her chair.

They returned to the bus to find a policeman stood outside, tall, greying and serious-looking. Both Penny and Eleri went up to him with poker faces before Eleri smiled.

Eleri: "Anything we can help you with officer?"

Police Guy: "I was just admiring your bus, seeing that you've made it into a campervan. I like the painting of the woman with the ravens on the front and sides too. I wouldn't mind doing the same, although I'd probably not have the painting. I retire soon, always liked camping too. Have you any useful tips for renovating?"

Eleri laughed: "It's about who you know. A friend gave me the bus, then another few friends are good on the practical side of things for renovations and paintings. Where would you like to go in it when you retire?"

Police Guy: "I love Scotland, Glen Coe and the North West, great landscapes and mountains, and it's quiet too, you can lose yourself up there. Can park where you like pretty much too, and camp, not like down here. We've got different laws in place in England, not as free as the Scots. They must be a great friend to give you it. Where are you two heading?"

Eleri: "I've friends who have a big bit of land in Devon. We'll be aiming to stay with them for a bit of time."

Police Guy smiled: "That sounds a lovely plan, I'm jealous. Well done with your bus home, and I hope it does you proud."

Penny: "Thanks a lot officer, so do we."

Eleri gave Penny a flat look as they boarded the bus.

Penny: "Glad he wasn't keen on an inspection of the interior."

Eleri: "That definitely wouldn't have been a laughing matter, he seemed friendly though."

They had as much fuel as they needed and, before they knew it, they had arrived at the campsite Eleri had booked them into. It was quiet because of the time of the year. Bella Vista campsite in the Chiltern Hills, an area of outstanding natural beauty by all accounts, but obviously not a patch on North Wales. There were only four other tents in the large field, and Eleri drove the bus to a quiet corner well away from anyone else. Hearing another car pull into the campsite she stared out at it as it swung towards them but then, thankfully, went to the far end of the field. It looked a small car, not the sort you'd find police driving.

Once they were set up for the night, they opened a bottle of Casillero Del Diablo and got stuck into the quiche Bryony had made them, which was full of goats cheese, pine nuts and broccoli. It made them go quiet until they'd polished it all off.

Sitting back in a bus chair with a glass of wine in hand, Eleri turned to Penny.

Eleri: "You all set for tomorrow?"

Penny: "I am, I know what I have to do and when."

Eleri smiled at her friend and was glad she wasn't doing this on her own. The wine made her feel a little giddy and she felt that her and Penny's lives had been leading up to this point, fated perhaps. The years of work and study, being with people on the sharp end of immoral decisions, the anguish of her family's trauma, Penny's deterioration in quality of life and, more recently, their plan which they'd worked on together over the past few months.

Eleri felt no regret for things she'd not done. No other path felt right to her; all other options to not take on the culprits felt like apathy and giving up. Watching the culprits get away with it with impunity again and again, and continuing to listen to their lies was not an option. The energy which had been building in her needed venting.

Eleri: "We'll leave here for 10am, it's just over an hour to London but it will give us plenty of time. The speeches are being given on the Pavilion at 12pm bang on, and we don't want to miss that."

Penny: "We'll be there. I'm going to hit the sack soon though, it has felt a long few weeks."

Penny sipped the last of the wine from her glass, wheeled back along the bus a few metres to the mattress and skilfully manoeuvred her way out of her chair and onto the mattress, pulling the duvet over her. She started snoring lightly within minutes.

Eleri had one more glass of wine before joining Penny. The wine made her fall into a slightly fevered sleep, sometimes coming awake for a while. She had various dreams whilst asleep and when she was awake the fears and doubts which didn't exist during the light of day crept in.

Should they be doing this? Why couldn't they stay quiet and get on with societal norms? She thought back to Smiler's words, but Eleri managed to beat the doubts down soon after they popped up. The evidence of the damage the culprits had done, and would continue to do, was all she needed to bat the doubts away.

In her first dream, she dreamed she was back as a child at the anti-war protest in Iraq with all her family. She flitted from there into being a child in Iraq, hiding as monumental blasts shook the building she was in. She flitted again to being held in her mother's arms as a bunch of hard-looking men came and took her father away. One of the men had extremely cold, steely-blue eyes and looked like he didn't like what he was doing, but Eleri was sure she'd not be seeing her father again. The cold-eyed man and Eleri looked at each other with some strange understanding passing between them. Eleri came awake listening to Penny's quiet snores. She vaguely thought she saw smoke coming from somewhere in the bus and couldn't remember lighting up herself, but was too tired to think on it.

When she fell asleep again, she was shocked even in her dream to be a young man at some kind of boarding school. She was in a dorm and a few kids were stood around one of the beds and started to punch a boy who let out a muffled cry. Eleri, as the young man, hated it, but was worried if she said anything that she'd be the next target. She went into a bathroom in the morning, looking in the mirror, hating the person who stared back, feeling lonely, lost and bewildered as to why the family in her dream had sent her to this horrible place. As other children came in, she put on a brave face and pretended everything was fine, even though she thought the place was a cesspit.

Eleri woke again, hand going to her forehead to wipe the sweat away. Penny still snoring, Eleri wished she could sleep as consistently as her friend. That last dream was bizarre. She had always believed anyone could change their lives around for the better and nobody was irredeemable, but she'd never thought about the culprits as being so. Surely even Freud would have seen them as a lost cause?

She drifted off once more into a dream she felt considerably more comfortable in. She was climbing with Osian and Lewis on the sea cliffs on Anglesey, on a climb called A Dream of White Horses, traversing above a huge sea arch. There was a golden light on the white quartzite rock and Eleri felt warmth towards both of her friends. The dream shifted slightly and it was just her and Osian at the top of the climb as the sun set, holding each other warmly, as the earth started to shake…

"Eleri! Eleri! Fuck, fuck, it's 10.30am, we've overslept!"

Penny's strong hands shook Eleri's shoulders up and down.

CHAPTER 16 - Y MORRIGAN

Judas looked around the Pavilion at the 'people' he was protecting, if indeed they were from the same genus, it looked like a form of devolution had been acting pretty fast on these culprits. Soon they'd be taking it in turns to sprout some complete bullshit to the masses. The weather suited Judas' mood well; cold, breezy and damp. He was dressed in dark jeans, a fleece and a black waistcoat for which he was thankful. His face was smooth and chiselled, unlike his current state of mind.

Only him and another security guy, Mark, were up on the Pavilion but there were guards arrayed around it and plenty more around the Parade Ground and park. They were checking for weapons and odd behaviour, although it didn't look like many people would be coming to see these prunes talk. Judas surveyed them all with his very cold, very bored eyes. The Pavilion itself was just a raised platform about a body and a half in height with a large banner back it with the festival blurb wrote large upon it.

He'd done some things for his country which had left a deep mark upon him and, looking at the current people he was working for, made him question his past and what he'd done. He'd done terrible things one shouldn't do to other people, because he had believed in his country, thinking it was great and its cause was one for good, at the time. But looking at who he was working for, people who lied and misled every day, made him call into question his past. And he didn't like it, not at all.

He had blood on his hands, and as much as he had tortured them, it tortured him more to think back on it all. He had been assured they had vital information, but his efforts had not been rewarded with anything of use. Instead, the sounds and images from those times would often haunt him.

He used to be able to tell himself that he respected how everything was run, but in recent years he'd found it harder to force this mindset. He wondered how his counterparts in other parts of the world felt, people protecting pigs, lying and divisive pigs doing no good. Did they feel shame like him?

He'd once thought that the country you were from made some kind of difference, and he'd seen himself as a true patriot. As Judas had gotten older, he'd begun to think that people were the same wherever you found them, most of them looked pretty much the same, had similar desires and dreams, no matter where someone came from or what language they spoke.

But here he was on a Pavilion, overseeing the protection of 'people' who had used hatred to spark a feeling of xenophobic superiority throughout the nation, blaming immigrants for woes they themselves had often caused, making minds smaller, throwing up barriers and making a big deal out of relatively small differences between people who were born on a different bit of land to them. Idiotic, wasteful and dangerous. Super privileged, entitled pigs, all of them having a background in deeply immoral behaviour, thought Judas, as he looked across the Pavilion.

"All clear!" He heard in his earpiece. As if he gave a fuck. He looked out with disgust and an element of pity at the small crowds of people beginning to form to listen to the drivel which awaited them. This is what his fucking country had come to, simpletons sucked in by immoral and deeply privileged morons. The world most days seemed a shit shade of grey to Judas nowadays and this particular day wasn't looking to be any different.

As he watched the inbred toads preen and prattle amongst themselves he dreamed about a meteorite coming down and ending all their farcical existences. Judas had never been one to rely on luck though and had given up on god, other than a desire to put a bullet in the fucker if he did exist. Imagine creating so much misery. Dawkins was right, if god did exist he was the greatest shitface there ever was.

And so Judas started his day, clearly not the most upbeat member of the Festival of Bullshit.

*

Eleri groggily woke up, realising that Penny was shaking her, and then Penny's words dripped into her mind. How the fuck had they both overslept on the day they'd been prepping for for months!?

Eleri: "Fuck! Sorry Penny. Let's hit the road, we'll still get there on time."

Eleri gave Penny a hand into her chair and they both went up front. Putting the keys into the ignition, Eleri turned the key and the engine made a spluttering sound briefly, then went quiet. The same happened the next five times she tried it between rests. Her face flushed and she was struggling to think straight.

Eleri: "Fuck, fuck, fuck. It was working fine the last few weeks, what is going on now?"

She went out of the door and gave the front of the bus a few kicks, looking into the Morrigan's painted eyes as if it were her fault. It was a chilly morning, breezy, drizzling and grey. Eleri's hands went to her head and pulled at her hair, thinking about what to do and having flashbacks to the shit times she'd had in her old Escort.

Penny: "Eleri, I think we left the lights on last night. We might just need a jump start."

Eleri ran towards the farmhouse that ran the campsite and,

after a slightly panicked chat with Dee who ran the show, her partner Ned to come out with jump leads. He was a huge guy and looked like he could have pushed the bus out of the field on his own. After a lot of revving of Ned's pickup, with Eleri pumping the accelerator, the bus eventually started up.

Eleri gave Ned a wave of thanks and her, Penny and the bus meandered out of the field as fast as they could. When they were back on the motorway, Eleri put her foot down and tested the max speed of the bus.

Eleri: "We'll be doing well to hit it for 12pm. Let's hope their speeches are going to drone on for a while."

Penny looked calm, a feeling Eleri was finding hard to grasp this morning, especially after sleeping badly and the rushed start.

As they sailed onto the Westway at 12.10pm, she eased off the accelerator. It would be something else to get pulled so close to their quarry. As they rounded on the A5 after a minute or so, they could see the edge of their destination, Hyde Park.

Penny got to work and slotted the metal side barriers that Osian had made into place on the side windows.

Hyde Park was mainly surrounded by trees but there were a couple of open areas. Eleri had decided to go via the circular water fountain feature halfway down on the east side just off the A4202 which would lead them right into the Parade Ground in Hyde Park.

Risking a glance into the park to see where they'd soon be aiming, she saw that the sods had set the Pavilion up next to the Reformers' Tree. How inappropriate, Eleri thought, a tree to commemorate protestors campaigning to give all adult men the right to vote and these lot thought to have their Festival of Bullshit over it, metaphorically pissing on the history of the past. The Pavilion looked to be 2 metres off the ground, 20 metres across and 5 metres wide, with around ten people on top of it.

As soon as Eleri had the bus level with the water feature on the A4202, she dropped the bus into second gear, revved the fuck out of it and broke through the metal barrier. She manoeuvred the bus around the large fountain bowl and accelerated again to ensure they had the velocity for smashing through another metal barrier which had been put up to encircle the Festival. The few people nearby wisely kept the hell out of the way.

In a matter of seconds of leaving the main road, they smashed through the last barrier blocking access to the park and found themselves slowly rolling in first gear towards the Pavilion. There was a crowd of a few hundred who got out of the way as the bus threatened to run them over. It all seemed too easy and Eleri risked a smile at Penny as they neared their quarry.

The people stood on top of the Pavilion were hard to make out at first, but as the bus neared Eleri and Penny were able to make them out. It was much like in her dreams.

There they all were, all of the culprits:

The king pig liar and his top few crony pigs,

The clever pig, Dim,

The posh disaster capitalist pig, who had made his millions on the misery of others,

The smug pigs who'd done so much damage,

The mad king of the snakes, even. What the fuck he was doing there? Eleri had no idea, but she couldn't believe her luck. They had them all, almost.

There were a couple of normal-looking people Eleri didn't recognise who must have been security, although one did look somewhat familiar. More of them could be seen in the parting crowd too. Eleri put down the barrier on the front window and went into the back to start the generator.

The culprits on the Pavilion looked to the bus, eyeing the painted figure of the Morrigan. They looked at each other, eyebrows raising, the smug pigs looking extra smug and the king of the pigs smirking like he was known for doing.

Eleri got together at the front of the bus with Penny and spoke into the microphone to test it.

"Hello!" Her voice blasted out of the speakers loudly.

"If any of you fucking pigs move, we are going to blow up every last one of you!" Penny's voice bellowed out to the culprits on the Pavilion.

Eleri gave Penny a flat stare, wishing she'd not played Fun Loving Criminals on the way down.

Eleri: "My friend is correct. Anyone on the Pavilion, please don't move. This bus is loaded with enough explosives to take out most of the park. They are relics from World War Two, but be sure I've tested that they still work. We just want to talk to you."

The crowds quickly got the idea that being in the area was a poor plan and the security teams started to get rid of the crowds as fast as was possible. The people on the Pavilion looked bewildered.

The king of the pigs took up the speaker's section of the podium and spoke to the bus.

"Oink, oink, oink," which meant; '*what do you want?*'

He didn't sound worried.

Eleri took a few seconds to settle herself before continuing.

Eleri: "We want to have a chat with you and the other people who are on the Pavilion; the people who have been making the decisions the last few years. Please come into the bus and take a seat."

The pig king looked to Judas, his eyes asking, "what should we do?"

Judas spoke into his mouth piece: "Stand down Mark, I'll go in with them and see what they have to say. I think we should believe what they say about the munitions, let's take them seriously. Everyone else clear the park."

Mark got off the Pavilion, putting distance between himself and the bus.

Judas spoke loudly to the culprits: "I guess we'll go in and talk with them, if you can tell them we are coming in slowly, please, sir."

Pig king: "Oink, Oink, Oink," which meant they were all coming in slowly.

Judas was intrigued by what was going on and was very curious as to who was inside the bus. Were they bluffing? It sounded like two women, but were there more people inside? Was it a few nutty environmental bods who were happy to spend the rest of their lives in jail? The woman's face painted on the bus with the raven shoulders would do them little favours when they were rotting in prison.

Judas gestured to the culprits to make their way off the Pavilion and into the bus entrance. He whispered in a voice they could all hear: "Do not do anything stupid gentlemen. Keep calm and do what they say."

On the outskirts of Hyde Park the blue Panda rolled to a stop next to the water fountain. It had been following Eleri and Penny's bus since the campsite in the Chilterns, but Lewis didn't want to risk his car any further. It was already parked illegally.

Zoe: "What the fuck are they up to?"

She stepped out of the little car, looking at where the bus had crashed through a tall metal barrier. She knew Bryony would go nuts at Lewis if she found out they were together. It had been a rough night with four of them sleeping in the car in the campsite, a pretty last-minute plan. Osian had got them all together, worried about what Eleri and penny might be up to.

Osian: "I told you she needs help. I'm certain it wasn't fireworks she was playing with in the quarry."

He sounded panicked and full of concern, forehead crunching down into his face.

Lewis had thought about how grief can change people, but he hadn't imagined it going quite so far with Eleri. It was clear her and Penny were going to extreme lengths on whatever it was they were up to. He didn't say anything as he stepped out of the car. Osian was right to organise this small team of friends to follow Eleri and Penny, but Lewis thought it might be too late.

Isabelle pushed open the final door, hair in a wild state and having flashbacks to the fear she'd had when Eleri detonated the gunpowder when they were children, but her feelings now were totally off the scale. Her normal easy smile was missing, but she gave Osian's arm a squeeze.

Isabelle: "We should go look through the gap she's made."

She wasn't sure she wanted to see what was going on, but they'd come this far.

They crept up to the gap and peered through, wondering if there was anything they could do. They could make out a lot of the people who had been stood on the Pavilion making their way onto the bus, but were too far away to hear whatever the speakers on the bus were saying. Every single one of them couldn't believe what was going on, what they were seeing.

Lewis lit a spliff and started puffing away in an attempt to calm his nerves, sometimes glancing back at his little car to make sure it was ok.

The culprits and Judas stepped into the bus, the culprits walking in two by two, glancing at the woman in the wheelchair with ginger hair and the woman with dark wavy hair and glasses as they went past. They looked around the bus expecting to see some men somewhere. Both the women held Mills bomb grenades and Judas clocked the compartments holding munitions halfway down the bus, it dawning on him that they were serious after all. Thank fuck for that, he thought, wondering if his daydreams about a meteorite had been answered by these women and this bus.

There were ten culprits and Judas in all, with Judas sitting behind them and the others facing the women, squashed into the small space. Judas ignored the group of people he despised, and yet seemed to be a part of, and studied the women. He judged them to be both in their 30s, one looked to be wheelchair bound with strong-looking hands, and the other reminded him of the figure painted on the front of the bus, some kind of a raven princess. He hoped to hell she wasn't totally crazy. Both women looked calm to Judas which, whether they were mad or not, gave him a level of respect for them.

Eleri and Penny looked at the culprits and the man who clearly didn't want to be associated with them, who was sat further back on his own. Eleri thought she recognised him from somewhere but she couldn't quite recall where. Only a few metres from them to the right, the pig king and the king of snakes sat next to each other, both smirking. Close up they were just how Eleri imagined them to be, you could literally feel their untrustworthiness in the air. On the other side sat the two smug pigs who had brought about great damage to so many. Behind the pig king sat his clever pig helper and then, in no particular order, sat some of the top pigs who had brought about austerity and division, leaving a wake of shittiness behind them, and who Eleri lay blame upon for Jordan's death.

Eleri: "So, thank you for joining us. We came here because we wanted to ask you some questions, something like an interview. We'll be live streaming these questions and your answers onto YouTube."

The smug pigs smiled at each other, smugly.

Penny put her grenades to the side, near her milkshake, before turning on her camera and pointing it toward all the culprits.

Eleri: "First question. The Trussell Trust says that 40% of the people using its foodbanks are due to delays or changes in their benefit payments and sanctions, another 40% due to classic signs of poverty, low incomes, debt and homelessness. How do you feel about that legacy? That's for you two, the smug ones."

Smug Pig 1: "I believed I was doing what was best for the country as a whole."

Smug Pig 2: "There was no magic money tree and I thought it was good that society was charitable enough to provide the foodbanks."

Penny's cheeks flushed at their answers, remembering her times down at the foodbank and thinking of the hunger that she and others she had met had experienced.

Eleri: "Well, what you two did clearly *wasn't* what was best for the country, was it? And it has become very clear as more and more millionaires and billionaires are appearing and making more profit than ever that there is, in fact, a magic money tree!"

The BBC had got a helicopter in the air and had also tracked down the YouTube link Penny had put out. They were filming from above, looking down on the bus, and also linked into the interview going on inside. In Deiniolen, Ray and Gwawr were watching and, after not speaking for many years, Gwawr whispered, "What the fuck?". In Caernarfon, Megan had opened up the envelope Eleri had given her with thousands of pounds of cash in, and also whispered, "What the fuck?". Some of the most corrupt hacks, editors and unscrupulous think-tank boffins were watching the television and realised the card they'd received in the post with eyes and raven wings on the front must be linked, faces going white, wondering if karma had finally come calling. Like an epiphany, most of them suddenly reflected on what they'd been doing, on how seriously bad it was, and they looked at the television wondering what was going to happen.

Eleri: "Ok, let us move onto question two. Many of you have children. Child poverty has gone up substantially over the last few years; hundreds of thousands more are now living in poverty, and many more people with a disability are now also living in poverty. The numbers were going down until you lot were put in charge of things. Come to think of it, there are now millions more people who would now be classed as *poor* because of you. Have you anything to say about this?"

"Oink, oink, oink," said the Pig King, which Eleri ignored as, whatever he meant, she knew all too well that it would be detached from any truth.

Eleri: "Anyone else?"

"Sssss, ssss, sssss," chipped in the King of the Snakes, which meant; "*it was down to more foreigners coming over and making our children poorer by stealing their parents' jobs*".

"It wasn't their fault, but that of their predecessors, and there really wasn't any money to help the children," chipped in the smug pigs together.

Eleri: "It seems clear that there *can* be money to help. Many countries manage it through a fair tax system, allowing them to have high quality health and social care. Foreigners also make up a fair amount of our health and social care workers; we'd be screwed without them! You blame immigrants for everything."

Penny kept the camera steady on whichever of the culprits was speaking.

Judas listened with interest, the women's questions and the shit answers being given chimed with his thoughts about the immoral nature of the current so-called 'leaders'. He was quite enjoying it so far, watching them squirm.

Eleri: "Ok, question three. You say that there isn't any money.

But all of you have money in corrupt offshore accounts. Tens of millions of pounds between you is stored there, maybe more, for the primary reason to avoid the tax laws in this country. Yet you had the gall to push austerity, and reduce tax for the rich, which hit the poorest in society the most. Do you feel any shame for your actions? That's to you smug pigs again."

The King of the Pigs smirked sideways at the smug pigs, feeling let off the hook.

"Oink, Oink, Oink, Oink, Oink, Oink, Oink, Oink, Oink, Oink, Oink," the smug pigs broke over each other defensively. Which meant it was their money in the offshore account and everything was kosher with it. The bankers worked really hard so deserved to keep their bonuses. Why would they feel any shame?

Eleri: "Well, many of you get shown in a certain Hollywood movie showing how profoundly corrupt these offshore accounts are, so it clearly isn't all kosher. As we've established, it appears to me that there *is* a magic money tree, which you have all been hiding."

Judas shook his head at the pathetic answers and asked Eleri if he could steal a rollie, to which she politely answered yes, and got the pigs to pass him one down.

Eleri: "Question four. You all cut the funding for the NHS, which has led to longer waiting times, fewer beds, and intense pressure on many people who are working in the NHS. As the population has aged, you've also given no thought to social care, so our parents and grandparents will all be stuffed and more likely to suffer misery in old age. Some of you promised more money for it, but didn't bother with delivering it. It's something essential for tens of millions of people here in the UK. Why do you want power when you are doing these terrible things? Wouldn't it be better having people in power who look after these essential institutions? You could all just retire on the vast wealth you've got hidden and leave these things to people who care about them, who are invested in them."

"Sssssss, ssssss, sssssss," piped up the Snake King, which meant; *"It's due to foreigners coming over and burdening the health care system".*

"Oink, oink, oink, oink, oink, oink," clamoured all of the pigs. This meant all sorts of things, from nobody being cleverer than them, to the fact that privatisation is very efficient, that it was the NHS managers fault, not theirs, and that people should really be paying for it, and that there was a need to lower taxes for our rich friends.

Eleri put her hand up to shush the pure nonsense they were spouting, feeling disappointed, although unsurprised.

Eleri: "People already are paying for it, through their taxes, and poorer people often seem to end up paying more tax, whereas the wealthy find loopholes to avoid it, such as yourselves! Let us move on."

"Question five. Most of you have received money from some far-right organisations in America, who have an agenda of pushing policies around climate change denial, denying women's rights to abortion, reducing worker rights, attacking trade unions and protestors, reducing environmental regulation and allowing increased pollution. I could go on, but you get the picture. You've all been helping to make the world, and in this case our little area of the world, a much shitter place. Do you regret getting your hands dirty with such dark money and pushing such immoral policies?"

There were quiet, furtive oinks from most of the pigs. Eleri knew they didn't like that good journalism could find out what their dirty secrets were, and who was paying them to do what.

The pigs wouldn't answer this question, but the King of the Snakes seemed very comfortable with the far-right agenda.

"Sssssss, sssss, sssssss," he purred, which meant he'd love more far-right policies to be pushed.

Eleri: "Right, so most of you are staying quiet on that one. And you, monsieur snake, it's been made clear that you are like a Nazi in modern day politics, often backing up racists and even genocidal maniacs. You have some amount of bad karma to be honest."

The king of the snakes sneered back, unfazed, comfortable with how big of a cunt he really was.

Eleri: "Number six. This one is a relatively minor one, but call it something of a 'bite-me'. We all know you've all done drugs, some of you are clearly high right now. But you are always outrageously hypocritical and love to announce war on drugs. You state that the crime that occurs is the buying and selling, when it's within your power to legalise it and help stop it destroying lives. Your prohibitions have clearly led to more deaths, as there is a lack of regulation and advice. Why this hypocrisy? After all, using ecstasy has a lower mortality risk than drinking alcohol, and is several levels lower than smoking tobacco, which you so kindly allow."

She blew out smoke from her rollie to punctuate her point.

"Sssssss, ssssss, ssssss," said the Snake King, which meant; "*drugs are being pushed by foreigners*".

"Oink, oink, oink, oink, oink, oink," clamoured all of the pigs, which meant anything from multiple assurances that they'd never done any drugs, to saying that it was illegal for a reason, that it couldn't work, that people wouldn't stand for the immorality.

The Pig King just rubbed his nose and Eleri could make out a small smudge of coke on the side of his nostril.

Eleri drew smoke in off her rollie and blew it out with a smile.

Eleri: "I'm starting to get the picture. Many of you have strong links with the alcohol and tobacco industry incidentally. Alcohol is the biggest killer of working-age adults in the UK and tobacco still kills more than 70,000 people per year in the UK, and maims many more."

"Ssssss, sssss, sssss," and "oink, oink, oink," which meant; *"nanny state".*

Eleri: "We wouldn't want the nanny state saving lives and reducing the profits for any of our friends, for sure. There aren't too many more questions, you'll be glad to hear."

Eleri finished her cigarette and peered through her glasses at the culprits, slightly shaking her head at the fact that some of these people had been put into such positions of power, such shallow, moronic fools. That anyone wanted to listen to any of them was beyond her, they had nothing of substance in their minds.

Eleri: "Number seven. What about the lying? Day in, day out. Fibs all the time. Fibs about money for the NHS when you've been screwing it, fibs about foreigners, fibs about how great you'll make things for people, while simultaneously taking away their services. Fibs, fibs, fibs, all the damn time. Have you any truths you'd like to tell us?"

"Oink, oink, oink," lied the Pig King, which meant he'd never told any porkies. Dim sniggered behind him and the others smirked quietly.

Eleri lit another rollie as the culprits went quiet again. She glanced at her middle finger with its yellow stain on the left side where she'd been holding the cigs. She'd only had that a few times in her life, notably when she was highly stressed. Then it was easy to end up smoking a lot.

Eleri: "Look. The reason for these questions is that me and my friend Penny here have been on the sharp end of some of the actions you set into play. One of us has had to go hungry for some time and has been going to a foodbank. Any of you ever used one?"

The culprits gave shakes of their heads in disdain, looking down their noses at Penny as she squinted back at them.

Eleri: "We thought not. One of us also lost someone dear to us, someone whose life deteriorated when they lost their job, due to cuts made by yourselves."

"Oink, oink, oink," laughed the culprits on the front seats; the smug ones, the Pig King and the Snake King. This just meant that they couldn't believe the little women could blame them for their actions. Behind them, the clever pig had started to look nervous, looking at the darkness developing behind him and at the faces of the two women.

Penny: "Let's stop the show."

She stopped streaming the footage and put the camera to one the side. The laughter from the culprits eventually stopped.

Eleri and Penny had certainly not expected the culprits to be vulgar enough to laugh at the reasons for the interview. They seemed an ugly bunch indeed and the interview really had firmed up in Eleri's mind that she'd made the right choice. The culprits were all gods of inequality.

"Oink, oink, oink," said the King of the Pigs, which meant; *"who is the woman on the front of the bus?"*

Eleri looked at his smug, dishonest face for a few seconds before answering.

Eleri: "That's the Morrigan, a dark Celtic goddess of fate, war, death, protection and," Eleri paused for a few seconds and blew out a puff of smoke. "Of retribution."

The pigs in the front chuckled. They didn't believe in retribution, if you had money and power you could prevent retribution from occurring more often than not. They believed they could do anything they liked with total impunity. The laws for the little people didn't apply to them.

Eleri ignored the chuckles, picked up and unrolled the pencil drawing from her old bedroom of the Morrigan.

Eleri: "This is it, I was brought up with stories about this creature. You know, you might say it helped inspire me to come down here and pay you a visit."

Judas' mind had been working itself up from its less-than-upbeat thoughts from earlier in the day. The culprits had tried in vain to answer the questions in a satisfactory manner but they had just reinforced what every sane person already knew, that they were all utter shites. Judas watched Eleri's face darken and their eyes met. They seemed to understand each other. The Pig King, his employer, looked to be up to something, and Judas was feeling mightily unimpressed with him and the other culprits.

*

The footage from inside the bus had stopped but, high above, the BBC helicopter saw a hummer-type vehicle drive right up to the bus door. It stopped there for a minute, then drove off, with some sort of music coming from the bus. A journalist on board the helicopter gave some commentary on the event unfolding.

BBC journalist: "It looks like a large Hummer vehicle has just left the bus having been there for a minute or so, it's making its way Eastward across the park. We are not sure who if anyone is on board, the Hummer was parked door to door with the bus and we've lost contact from inside. No more questions have been streamed in the last few minutes."

Time seemed to slow down.

"Non, rien de rien" Could vaguely be heard far below.

BBC journalist listened carefully before asking quizzically: "Is that Edith Piaf?"

The Hummer started to pick up speed and got about a hundred metres from the bus.

The BBC camera zoomed in onto the image of the Morrigan on the front of the bus.

CHAPTER 17:
NEWID (CHANGE)

B

O

O

M

The helicopter shook from the huge blast and only just stayed in the air. Below, chaos reigned. The camera came back to focus on the ground below and people all over the world looked down to where they'd once seen the top of the bus, only a 50-metre wide crater remaining. A Raven flew out of the smoke, somehow evading the blast wave. Smoke was everywhere and the sirens of police, ambulances and fire engines could be heard. There was a smell in the air akin to that of bacon crisps.

BBC Reporter: "My god. They weren't bluffing, they've blown up the bus and a fair bit of Hyde Park. Shit."

Lewis, Zoe, Isabelle and Osian stepped out from the smoke and walked back towards the Panda, faces grey from dust and shock. They got back into their car, Osian in tears, before Lewis got them on the road. Eleri and Penny were gone. They set off back to North Wales in silence, trying to take in what they'd seen.

The following days wore on slowly after the Festival of Bullshit had been rudely hijacked. Of the culprits there was no sign, the vehicle that had gone near the bus was a remote and had got clear of the blast but was empty, and all of the bus's occupants were presumed to have been obliterated in the blast. All that could be seen in the immediate aftermath was chaos and dust.

But there was a tangible change now the culprits were gone, like a warning shot had been fired across the heads of would-be immoral leaders. People didn't know if they were dreaming as events unfolded, or if it was some kind of mushroom utopia.

Whether it was right or wrong for the culprits to have been

obliterated is a question few people asked. It was clear some of the culprits would have caused a coup or riot to maintain power if they thought they had a chance to get away with it, some had even supported other world leaders who had attempted to do so. Few criminals in the history of the world had managed to do as much damage, perhaps only the biggest names involved in genocidal dictatorships, so they clearly had it coming to them.

With this in mind, the leaders who stepped into the breach thought it best to have a completely different approach, such as telling the truth rather than lying. They didn't use divisive, hateful language as, in their heart of hearts, they knew everyone was the same and deserved the same respect, although perhaps people in Cwm-y-Glo were slightly cooler. The new leaders were concerned about all people and felt responsibility for the actions they made. They also didn't want a bus full of explosives and pissed-off people coming their way, which added an incentive to not act like daft pigs.

They started to tax the profits of the richest which helped to pay for services for everyone. It was in everyone's interest, they said, because the rich won't notice and the world their children will grow up into will be fairer and less likely to kill them or make them miserable.

"A fair tax on the rich allows better education, health and social services for everyone, meaning everyone will get a fair chance in life and people won't be worried about being left alone and lonely in shambolic care homes in old age. We'll create a green economy with the money so peoples' children and grandchildren won't be thoroughly ashamed of the awful decisions many adults have been making these last few years," said the new leaders.

The magic spell which appeared to be over the island of Britain that allowed it to be ruled by horrible pigs looked to have finally gone. People looked back at what the many different pig kings had said on the TV screen before they disappeared and wondered why they'd been given any power at all.

"Did we let them lead us?" asked the people of Britain.

"Why would we have done that?" People were shaking their heads at the lunacy of the idea.

And nowhere in the land of Britain was the Pig King's leadership missed, for it was clearly full of lies, deceit, division, and wasted money and time. Although their families did mourn them, they had no friends who did so. Only people of very kind spirit did excuse them by pointing to the shitty childhoods they must have had, as well as a lack of love and being brainwashed into thinking they were better than anyone else. The profoundly corrupt hacks and editors who'd helped ferment racism and hate on behalf of their billionaire bosses did resign from their jobs, knowing they'd been acting like pieces of shit and felt lucky not to have been atomised in the crater with the bus.

Around the crater itself, some people did lay toy buses as a token memorial, but nobody really knew if it was to the people who brought the Bus of Retribution, as it had become known, or if they were related to some of the many promises broken by the culprits. A large slate gravestone also arrived at the crater with austerity, entitlement & bigotry engraved in large writing across the stone. Eventually, when the crater had been filled in and the grass had regrown, the area was set up as a lovely area for immigrants to rest, and outdoor learning and physical activity sessions were set up for them, although some did mention that when the wind blew through the nearby trees it sounded like a snake hissing.

More widely, people from all over the world had been watching what had been going on. They had realised for some time that Britain had been led by amazingly stupid pigs. It had been something to offer a sad humour; Britain had been a sure contender for the country led by the thickest people in the world. But now they had managed to get rid of them and instead had leaders who tried to tell the truth and make fair decisions, and seemed to be improving people's lives rather than lining a few of their friends' pockets with gold.

A change seemed to be brewing.

CHAPTER 18: Y DIWEDD (THE END)

Back in the county of Gwynedd, Eleri's friends had made their way back to their homes after the fateful trip to Llundain (London). Lewis went back to working in the Carneddau mountains to help clear his mind. Isabelle got her head down with her artwork, trying to forget about the painting of the Morrigan she and Maisy had put on the front of the bus. Zoe went back to the newspaper and tried to write stories which weren't as bigoted towards tourists and people who weren't born in Wales.

Poor Osian was inconsolable and went into himself and his work. He began many journeys to the quarries, deep into the slate hole of Mordor where he once saw Eleri let loose an almighty blast. He started to make a statue of Eleri out of a narrow fin of slate in the base of the great hole. Using his great skill, in only a matter of weeks there stood a haunting likeness of Eleri, complete with her glasses and a rollie in her mouth.

All of them had expected a visit from the police at some point, but as the weeks wore on, one never came. People reported sightings of the bus with a woman's face painted on it around Halloween, but the cops that weren't on strike were too dozy to work out where it had come from and figured whoever had driven it had perished in the huge blast. Besides which, they all thought that whoever had been in the bus had done them a favour. The police had hated working for little piggies who were happy to break the law and only ever got up to no good, making the police look bad.

Across most of Gwynedd there were celebrations of the fact that the total crooks who had belittled socialism, devolution and Wales in general had gone. People saw it as a karma much like that which many of the quarry owners of old deserved, those who treated so many so badly, thinking about their profits over people's lives. Those who had perished were just the modern version of the old bastards; people happy to see thousands of lives destroyed.

After a couple of months of solitude, Osian made his way round to see Lewis in Llanberis. It was a dreary day just before New Year and Osian told him of the statue he'd made in the quarries.

Lewis: "We should all go Osh. Me, Zoe and Isabelle would love to see it."

And on New Year's Day they did make their way into the hole, with booze and fags to celebrate their friends' lives. After a time getting tipsy and baked and spinning yarns about old times, Zoe looked up from the slate boulder she was sat on and noticed a figure standing in a quarry entrance, perched high in the rock face, looking down on them. It looked to be a slim person smoking, and there was a figure next to them who looked a lot shorter and wider.

They all looked up to where Zoe was looking.

"What the fuck?"

They quietly made their way back up some ladders and up to the tunnel where they'd seen the two figures near its end. They walked in through the dark tunnel for a time to where the two figures were silhouetted against the light. It was Thomas and Penny.

"Hello," the pair said at the same time. They were sharing a flask of peppermint and liquorice tea.

Zoe: "What happened? Where is Eleri?"

Thomas: "We got out, Eleri didn't."

He tapped the ash off the end of his rollie.

"How?" asked Osian and Isabelle, looking pasty-faced as Lewis took deep drags on a spliff.

Penny: "We stopped filming, not sure if you've seen the footage, as it was pointless getting answers from them. There was no self-awareness, remorse or shame. They were a lost cause."

Penny took up the story in the bus.

*

There was laughter from the pigs nearest to Eleri and Penny, although the smart pig began to look nervous, glancing from the women back towards Judas. Eleri's face darkened. She looked to Judas and an understanding passed between them; the judges were decided, the culprits sentenced.

At that moment BJ, heavily coked-up, leered at Penny, eyes squinting, hers squinting back at him. He leaned out of his chair and went for Penny with both hands, believing he was a heroic figure. Penny clasped his hands in hers in a game of peanuts and screamed into his fat, dishonest face. Eleri had a finger deeply through a grenade in one hand but with the other she reached for her brother's plaque and was about to clout BJ in the head. Before she was able to there was a soft thud and BJ grunted and slid off Penny, breathing hard and groaning.

The bus fell silent as everyone on it took in what had happened. Judas was stood up at the back with a silencer on a handgun and had just shot his boss in the shoulder.

"You fucking bunch of rotten, corrupt bastards!" Judas declared as he circled his gun between the culprits.

"You are all responsible for screwing this country. You do know that don't you? Lying all the time, pissed and high most of the time, blaming others for your inadequacies. Cutting services for the poorest whilst hiding your riches untaxed in Panama and such like. Promising complete bollox you know you cannot deliver. You fucking useless, cowardly, bastard fucks."

The culprits all cowered. Eleri and Penny looked at each other, eyebrows raised, wondering where events were going now. Judas looked so like the person Eleri had dreamed of, it felt even more surreal than the mad situation she and Penny had created.

Judas, whispering into his mouthpiece: "Mark, send in the unmanned Hummer, I may be able to get some civilians out."

As Judas was talking, the clever pig, Dim, had heard Judas' whispers and had quickly deduced that he and the other culprits were unlikely to be who Judas was thinking of saving. He lunged at Judas with a wicked thin knife, half a foot long, managing to stab deep into Judas' side. Judas' body clenched up in agony but he managed to let loose another six bullets as he grappled painfully with one hand against Dim. Two of the bullets flew true, blowing the heads off the smug pigs. Never again would they be offering misery to the masses.

Eleri was close to blowing everything to kingdom come when a figure, who had somehow stowed themselves onboard, made their way limping from the back of the bus and helped Judas fend off the clever pig. The stowaway knocked the knife from the culprits hand, punched him into the chair and managed to pull a badly injured Judas along the bus to where Eleri and Penny were sitting. It was Thomas.

How the fuck he'd managed to stowaway without them noticing him smoking, Eleri would never know, but she guessed nobody knew the bus as well as he did.

The remaining pigs gathered back around Dim, who had retrieved his knife, even the wounded BJ, although Dim pushed him aside like he was a trolley. The King of the Snakes made a play towards Penny but she chucked the dregs of her milkshake into his mean, bigoted, bastard face. It went down his green suit and he gurgled before retreating, like a foul ooze, back to the others.

The Hummer that Judas had ordered pulled up to the bus door.

The bus was then divided, much like light and darkness, with Eleri's team stopping the culprits from seeping back out into the world. The culprit side stood for lies, privilege, division and hate, whereas Eleri's side stood for hope, equity, community and of course, retribution.

Eleri: "Thomas, get Penny and Judas onto that Hummer".

She turned to Penny and whispered.

Eleri: "Change of plan, Penny."

She took up a blocking stance in the middle of the aisle, Jordan's heavy slate 'club' in one hand, two grenades in the other, looking every bit like the Morrigan pictured on the front of the bus. A raven queen, a queen of retribution. Few criminals in history had done as much damage as the ones she now faced.

Thomas quickly helped manoeuvre an uncertain-looking Penny onto the Hummer and dragged a near-unconscious Judas on with him. Thomas was on his way back into the bus when Eleri appeared in his face, pushed him hard and flicked the button on the door whence it immediately started moving, leaving a forlorn Penny and Thomas peering through a small window back towards the bus.

Inside the bus Eleri squared off to Dim and the others. Edith Piaf's 'No Regrets' song began to play through the speakers and Eleri wondered how the fuck that had come on.

Non, rien de rien

Non, je ne regrette rien

Ni le bien qu'on m'a fait

Ni le mal

Penny heard the music playing and whispered to Thomas: "What is that?"

Eleri faced Dim who, leading the remaining culprits, was looking particularly mean with his axe-like face sneering, thin wicked-looking knife out. Dim started edging towards Eleri with the other culprits, all cowering behind him. His dark eyes locked on Eleri's as he weaved his knife around in the air, starting to close the gap.

Dim: "Look, you can have these morons, but I want to get out. The world needs me. I'm the smartest person there has ever been. I can change things to run 1000 times more efficiently."

He wondered how committed his opponent was, whilst also thinking through the 'game theories' he'd been through in his head.

Eleri almost laughed at Dim's words as she chucked both her grenades over his head towards the munitions. Eleri was 100% certain Dim didn't deserve to get off the bus, and she was sure he was aware of this fact. Spinning around, Dim, who didn't have the best vision but whose reflexes were quick, somehow managed to get to both grenades. He went to throw them out of the door of the bus. He gave two sure throws which had both grenades arcing towards the open doorway.

Unfortunately for Dim and the other culprits, Eleri was there with Jordan's slate plaque in hand, the unearthly energy she'd had as a child coming back into play. With a rollie in her mouth, she skilfully batted both grenades back in quick succession towards the munitions store. One ricocheted off BJ's ear and the other hit Dim square in the forehead. The King of the Snakes, who had ingratiated himself with dictators and sowed division and hatred at any opportunity, howled as he saw his looming demise. Eleri smiled and felt the massive pressure in her mind which had been building for years finally release. Using Jordan's plaque to finish had felt like poetic justice. She took a deep drag on her rollie.

As the grenades set off, the other munitions also went off and the huge blast rocked the Hummer to buggery and Thomas was thrown back into Penny.

*

"I blacked out, and when I woke up we were on a helicopter being taken to some kind of safe house in the Lake District."

Thomas spoke slowly, taking drags on his rollie.

"They kept us there a month, seemed to be friends of Judas', though he was too screwed to speak much. Eventually they dropped us off in Deiniolen. We gave Ray and Gwawr a surprise. You know she has started talking again? Slowly, but it's a start. We've just been hanging out with them the last few days."

Lewis blew out a big exhale of weed.

Lewis: "So, Eleri really is gone then?"

Thomas: "It should have been me who got left behind, I don't have long left anyway."

Penny: "She knew what she was doing Thomas, she had a plan."

Thomas: "Quite the fucking plan."

They all looked down at Osian's statue in various states of sorrow, before eventually pouring out G&Ts and toasting to Eleri's life.

*

Someone was definitely dreaming or could it be that it was a fairy tale ending? The change that had been brewing did take hold around the world, with people from all countries taking a good look at their leaders. They thought about whether or not they told the truth, or if they mainly lied and sowed division to meet their own ends.

And in the countries that found they too had pigs ruling them, the people rose up, often behind the symbol of the Morrigan. They gave the pigs the choice of stepping down from power or facing a similar demise as was seen on the Retribution Bus. The would-be demagogues, dictators and economically illiterate cretins did think again before trying their dirty hands and pushing narratives based on ideology rather than evidence. Fucking feckless fucks for leaders around the world just disappeared and normal people with functioning brains took over and started to do a decent job. All countries signed up to an international, binding agreement by which no country would allow daft pigs to lead them ever again...

*

It was some months later that Osian and Lewis were exploring in the slate quarries and heard blasts in one of the holes and went in to investigate.

As they were walking along, Lewis got notifications on his phone with some seriously bad news. The NHS had collapsed, and most public services had been sold off to oligarchs who were getting rid of any workers' rights and who would pay everyone bugger all. There had been a riot a few days ago involving an insurrection-style coup led by horrible pigs, who had somehow got themselves into power to fuck everything up completely yet again.

Lewis: "Jesus Christ Osh, there is some bad shit going down."

They looked down from the tunnel leading into the chasm with the slate statue of Eleri, a raven perched on a slate boulder nearby looking up at them. Looking back through the tunnel where they'd just walked, a figure appeared, a shadow silhouetted against the light of the tunnel, small tendrils of smoke trailing behind their hand. Ravens flew past the figure through the tunnel, cawing.

Osian's and Lewis' eyebrows rose.

"How much acid did we just do Osian?" Lewis chimed as the figure got nearer.

AMEN

Printed in Great Britain
by Amazon

21127903R00122